THE BEAUTIFUL TRUTH

THE HOPE OF TOMORROW

Edited By Lynsey Evans

First published in Great Britain in 2025 by:

Young Writers
Remus House
Coltsfoot Drive
Peterborough
PE2 9BF
Telephone: 01733 890066
Website: www.youngwriters.co.uk

All Rights Reserved
Book Design by Ashley Janson
© Copyright Contributors 2024
Softback ISBN 978-1-83685-174-5
Printed and bound in the UK by BookPrintingUK
Website: www.bookprintinguk.com
YB0625R

Foreword

Since 1991, here at Young Writers we have celebrated the awesome power of creative writing, especially in young adults where it can serve as a vital method of expressing their emotions and views about the world around them. In every poem we see the effort and thought that each student published in this book has put into their work and by creating this anthology we hope to encourage them further with the ultimate goal of sparking a life-long love of writing.

Our latest competition for secondary school students, The Beautiful Truth, asked young writers to consider what their truth is, what's important to them, and how to express that using the power of words. We wanted to give them a voice, the chance to express themselves freely and honestly, something which is so important for these young adults to feel confident and listened to. They could give an opinion, highlight an issue, consider a dilemma, impart advice or simply write about something they love. There were no restrictions on style or subject so you will find an anthology brimming with a variety of poetic styles and topics. We hope you find it as absorbing as we have.

We encourage young writers to express themselves and address subjects that matter to them, which sometimes means writing about sensitive or contentious topics. If you have been affected by any issues raised in this book, details on where to find help can be found at
www.youngwriters.co.uk/info/other/contact-lines

Contents

Arnold Lodge School, Leamington Spa

A Donovan	1
Kasper	2
Remi Runciman (16)	4
Raphael Gregory (12)	5
Karam Lail (13)	6
Robin Sjurseth (12)	7
Freya Soni	8
Katie Burns (13)	9

Beaumont School, St Albans

Manel Hamouchi (11)	10
Martha Baker (17)	11
Evie Guyver (12)	12
Scarlet Nguyen (12)	13
Manel Hamouchi (11)	14
Isla Bailey (12)	15
Scarlett Parkin (13)	16
Mia Pisharody (12)	17
Estella Reid (12)	18

Blessed Thomas Holford Catholic College, Altrincham

Berenika Arciszewska (13)	19

Braeside School, Buckhurst Hill

Freya Foster (15)	20
Elysia Miller (12)	23
Angel Fearon (14)	24
Zaynab Khan (15)	27
Alexa Stead (15)	28
Amaya Uddin (15)	31

Dilly Roth (15)	32
Afaaf Faraz (13)	34
Siya Grewal Badesha (12)	36
Eliza Muneer (16)	38
Aiza Iftikhar (12)	40
Matilda-Rose Akeru (11)	41
Beatrice Neighbour (15)	42
Imaan Mir (12)	44
Yumnah Khan (14)	46
Lilly Kenee (13)	47
Shreeya Mehta (11)	48
Sadie King (11)	49

Brighton Hove & Sussex Sixth Form College, Hove

Josie Richards (17)	50
Samin Toofan (17)	52

Brockenhurst College, Brockenhurst

Taylia Edy (17)	53
Clobha Moffat (16)	54
Atlas Pollock (16)	55
Taylor Barnes (16)	56
Emerson Poole (17)	57

Chilton Bridge School, Chilton Cantelo

Jessica-Louise Adams (14)	58

Culford School, Culford

Oliver Spenser-Morris (16)	59

Esher College, Thames Ditton

Alistair Walker	61

Hans Price Academy, Weston-Super-Mare

Isabel Cooke (13)	63

Higham Lane School, Nuneaton

Valentina Ciechanowska (13)	64

King Edward VI High School For Girls, Birmingham

Aariya Kaur Bassi (11)	66
Serena Santra (11)	67

Langholm Academy, Langholm

Melinda King (12)	68

Lochgilphead High School, Lochgilphead

Cara Green (12)	69

Ludlow CE School, Ludlow

Liara Thomas-Lewis (11)	70

Manchester Islamic Grammar School For Girls, Chorlton

Sameera Ahamed (12)	71
Zaynab Ijaz (11)	72
Fatima Chaudhary (13)	74

Mount House School, Hadley Wood

Ava Sapani (12)	75

Newlands Girls' School, Maidenhead

Alicia Delacour (13)	77
Eleanor Franzen (12)	78
Holly Tooley (11)	79

Notre Dame Senior School, Cobham

Frida Macfarlane (11)	80
Savannah Greene (12)	81

Royal Latin School, Buckingham

Wahi Noor (16)	82

Rutlish School, Merton

Matthew Dix (15)	83
Alexander Harper (12)	84
Toni Bosch-Garcia (13)	86
Nickson Wamala (12)	87

Seaham High School, Seaham

George Emmerson (11)	88
Jessica Moon (11)	89
Lauren Blagden	90
Megan Westwood (11)	91
Lilly-Anne Laing (11)	92
Matthew Saville (11)	93

St Bees School, St Bees

Amisha Naurang (15)	94
Alice Gould (11)	95
Eve McMullan (16)	96
Suproto Mansur (17)	98
Imogen Freeman (12)	99

St Ninian's High School, Kirkintilloch

Eva Stirling (12)	100
Finlay McMaster (11)	101

St Philip Howard Catholic High School, Barnham

Lilly-Mai Unsted (14) 102
Niah Linard-Salter (11) 104
Stanley Brown (11) 106

Stantonbury High School, Stantonbury

Harley Parker (15) 107
Jemimah Mohammed (13) 109
Jannat Rashid (15) 111

The Castle School, Taunton

Lanie Hanbidge-Moore 115
Harvey Yarde (12) 116
Arlo Norbury (12) 118
Elliott O'Shea (13) 120
Mia Lewis 122
Olivia-Rose Wibrew (12) 124
Ava Taylor (12) 126
Viren Peter (12) 127
Alice Farmer (12) 128
Manny Ashley (13) 129
Amandine Playfair 130
Artie Townsend 131
Bella Snailham 132
Abigail Collings 133
Rosie Huxtable-Curno 134
Beatrice Nicholson (13) 135
Hannah Gilling (13) 136
Emerson Goss (13) 137
Gabriella Lawton (12) 138
Elena Kontopoulos 139
Hayden Yarde (13) 140
Josh Hawkins 141
Grace Walker 142
Lucy Bernard (13) 143
Edith Watson 144
Ned Parkes (12) 145
Amy Vautier (12) 146
Sebastian Ivan 147

Jesse Sweeting (13) 148
Kevin Dela Cruz 149
Arran McDonald (13) 150
Amber Biggs (12) 151
Joshua Griffiths (12) 152
Daniel Brown (12) 153
Alfie Prince 154
Lacey Bishop (13) 155
Zack Coles (13) 156
Anya Shearman (12) 157
Pippa Parrish (13) 158
Hayden McMurdo (13) 159
Frederick Paul 160
Mina Leslie 161
Alexander Hingley (13) 162
Annabelle Hall (12) 163

The John Roan School, Blackheath

George Hodgins (11) 164
Artem Baliuk (13) 166
Morgan Reynolds (11) 168
Zoja Woloszyn (13) 169
James Mac (15) 170
Rugile Kazakeviciute (13) 171

The Peterborough School, Peterborough

Aditi Sharma (13) 172
Avika Yadav (13) 174

The Vyne Community School, Basingstoke

Alina Jack-Price (16) 175

Thomas Keble School, Eastcombe

Lara Hopkins (13) 176

Twickenham School, Whitton

Javeria Kamran (11) 178
Emily Hall (13) 180

Chloe Ku (13) 181

Wellfield Community School, Wingate

Ocearna Harvey-Bullock (15) 182
Kaitlyn-Louise Gorton (12) 183

Wellington College, Belfast

Eleanor Goodwin (13) 184
Erin Carr (12) 186
Clara Toal 187

THE POEMS

FREEDOM

BELIEVE!

HONESTY

TRUTH

My Everyday Truth

My truth changes constantly,
Sometimes I feel like nobody understands me,
Sometimes I feel like I don't understand anybody,
Occasionally I feel like I don't deserve to be here,
Some of the time I feel like others suck my freedom away.
Sometimes I feel and embrace the warmth of my friends and family,
Every so often I want to express my creativity like a blooming flower,
Occasionally I want to learn, to dream, to achieve,
Most of the time I want to build a better place and be the best I can be.
I didn't used to want my truth to be everything it is.
But I realised that my beautiful truth is what makes me me, even when things get tough.

A Donovan
Arnold Lodge School, Leamington Spa

True To Myself

It was a long cold winter hiding down in the dark
With the grey clouds covering the sad blue sky
Thought that maybe it'd snow
But no
I had to let it go
Like all the other wishes I had for the wintertime.

It's just a lesson that I've learned
I should always give in return
For the sunny days and bright smiles that seem so hard to find
'Cause when you take away the lies all that's left is the truth
The truth that gives you wings
That lets you fly.

People putting on their fake faces every day to go to work, to school, to play
They just want to be liked and accepted
But they keep pretending to be what they're not
Every day, every day, every day, every day.

Don't keep pretending to be different than you are
Your true personality shines bright like a star
Don't keep trying to be more perfect than you are
(Shine bright like a star)
When you look inside the mirror,
What is it that you see?
A face full of lies, the truth, or reality?

Who you are is who you are
And it's who you're meant to be.

The truth is right here
And it's here to set you free.

I'll stay true to myself before anyone else
Will I find my beautiful truth?
I really can't tell
Am I finally going to come out of my shell?

Kasper
Arnold Lodge School, Leamington Spa

Dancing With The Devil

I never thought I'd dance with the devil.
I thought I'd be one of God's praised angels -
The ones with hair like gold lace and faces that held the sun's grace.

But now I know I'll never see Heaven's gate,
I don't even have a place.

I first saw the Devil at thirteen.
They didn't have horns or pointy teeth.
In fact,
She wasn't even a man.

She was beautiful - like an undying star in the sea of darkness,
But she wasn't mine.

Alas, no matter how much I tried to appease God, we never saw eye to eye.

Remi Runciman (16)
Arnold Lodge School, Leamington Spa

There In Front Of Me, I See...

There in front of me, I see the beauty,
The beauty of life
The beauty of everything around me.

There in front of me, I see the hatred,
The hatred of that self-loathing pit inside every person's soul, which eats away at their confidence.

There in front of me, I see hope,
The hope of a good life,
A little spark in a dark place that rightfully rebels against negativity, which cowardly hides behind that face of normality.

But in the end, there is always

A wish.

Raphael Gregory (12)
Arnold Lodge School, Leamington Spa

Untitled

There's nothing more ugly than dishonesty
I must tell you how much it displeases me
Sadness and anger disperse through the air
The streets are deserted, come out if you dare
Stories are told of our ruined kingdom
Children excited, like little minions
They are told about this so-called wondrous place
Until they set foot in here, disgusted by the look on their face
Have you heard of the truthful oppression
People are curious, they gossip like it's an obsession...

Karam Lail (13)
Arnold Lodge School, Leamington Spa

Untitled

With every song and rhapsody,
A brand-new birth of symphony,
From notes A to G I find my peace
Music that belongs to me,
It transports me to another place,
As I dance through raindrops, twirl across space,
An explosion of beauty burns in pace,
The music that takes me face-to-face,
The beat of time ebbs and flows,
Changing with me like a seed that grows,
It blossoms mighty, flowering strong,
The music, a beautiful truth that I long for.

Robin Sjurseth (12)
Arnold Lodge School, Leamington Spa

Hidden

Each layer hides it
Each layer protects it
Each layer, a sheet of pure, beautiful stone
Holds it close
A small grain of sand in the centre of a pearl.

The needle can scratch from time to time
But it fills up the room
Every song and every beat
Sometimes songs may end
And sometimes it may hurt.

Freya Soni
Arnold Lodge School, Leamington Spa

Friendship Is Love

Friendship is what the heart yearns,
Without friendship, you'll be lonely and won't learn,
If I don't see my friends my heart burns,
Without my friends, I'm a mess
But when I see them, I don't feel like I matter less.

Katie Burns (13)
Arnold Lodge School, Leamington Spa

Dream

D eep in my sleep, I wake up to a new world, where I belong. I don't have to change, I quite like that.

R acing across the world within seconds, visiting the places I've always wanted to go to. Feeling happy. If this is a dream, I don't want it to end

E scaping all my worries, forgetting the real world. Until I don't. I wake up, I have to.

A mazed at how fast it went and came, I am forced to get ready. I keep thinking, and thinking. And thinking. About my fate in their hands.

M y journey to the end of my time at Edgewater Secondary School is so close I can taste it. I really can't, but it feels like I can. As I walk down a corridor that feels like forever, I notice many eyes staring deep into my soul. Girls whisper with intensity. Boys huddle and shove. It's then and there I realise. They know. Everyone knows. I am done. Finished. Expelled.

Manel Hamouchi (11)
Beaumont School, St Albans

Sapien Elegy

I feel it.
Inside me.
It's the drum beating,
Conflagration of my heart, heating
Up, passion that roars and bellows
Like a bear in chains.
Remove these, and it would devour me for spite, so
Manacles digging into animal flesh, bright and stark,
Carving out those conditioned marks,
Crimson beacons that scream the faults of civilisation
Until rendered hoarse.
I feel as if it's that pain of wounds and squeals,
As the restrained creature reels
Within me.

My eyes leak acid, raw with burns,
Watch as the world churns
Through a blurred and tinted lens.
Remove this, and I would see their hands slick with blood,
As their nail-like claws hooked, virtuosic, around flesh.
Fresh; their helpless fellow monster,
Just as savage,
That they would bestially ravage,
If we were allowed to see desire.

Martha Baker (17)
Beaumont School, St Albans

Never Stop Dreaming

I have always had a desire to dance.
To stop thinking and prance.
When I was two I was diagnosed with arthritis.
It was hell now and then.
But I fought until I couldn't feel.
I joined a school dance, no one wanted me there.
I may not be a pretty face or hair but I try!
On the weekend my dad came, disappointed.
I quit boxing and joined dance.
I pursued my dream happy or sad.
It's not too bad.
I know I'm not there yet but soon I'll reach it.
I have always dreamed it!
Follow your dreams.
Take it from me!
Pick yourself up.
Proud and true.
Your dreams will come to you!
My dreams were on hold, I still fight arthritis.
But now I dance bold!

Evie Guyver (12)
Beaumont School, St Albans

One Fragment Of Hope

As a child I was told, there was no way to break free.
The omnipresent rule dominated over us all.
Everywhere you stepped, the smell of fear facaded the air.
I was kept in the dark, never saw anything except despair.
Every small window of hope, I tried to take,
But every chance was always smashed by them.
Their eyes, they had never shown compassion, a spark of warmth,
Never capable of love.
So if you try to hide,
Just be warned,
The only way to be human,
Is to love.
A fragment of hope among the dark,
Remember,
A robot is not alive.
I spread my wings and flew away,
To that window of hope.

Scarlet Nguyen (12)
Beaumont School, St Albans

My Reality

No one is safe
Not in this world
I have many regrets
Social media is one
I painted a picture of myself
But it wasn't true
It's what they wanted to see
It's what they wanted to believe
It's what I did
It's what I regret.

At last, I was one of them
The girls who put on make-up all the time
The girls who dated boys and acted like it was nothing
The girls who did TikToks and posted videos on Instagram
The girls who hated practically everyone
Everyone except me
They finally liked me
But did I like me?

Manel Hamouchi (11)
Beaumont School, St Albans

The Song Of The Free

Among the world of the caged,
Where birds cannot roam free,
One day the door flies open,
With endless possibilities.
But as you spread your wings to fly,
You find you cannot go up high.
Life in a cage keeps your wings closed,
So when you leave you cannot roam free
But only fall endlessly.
But one day you look up in the sky,
There's a single bird, flying up high.
So you study and try to fly up so high
To sing the song of the free.

Isla Bailey (12)
Beaumont School, St Albans

Identity, That's Me

I magine being able to look back on your life and say, "That's me."
D ancing like no one's watching, that's me
E ncouraging people when they're upset, that's me
N ot always knowing how to react, that's me
T eam player, that's me
I ndependent, but love company, that's me
T actile natured, that's me
Y ou can't change my identity, because, after all, that's me.

Scarlett Parkin (13)
Beaumont School, St Albans

Lost

Every soul the same
All doors closed
They never let you gain
Lost in the blue lights
Robots are your reality

When you feel different to the rest
On the inside and in your head
Lost in the blue lights
Robots are your reality

Everywhere you look
Minds are covered up with soot
Rights are wrong
Safe is nowhere
Lost in the blue lights
Robots are our reality.

Mia Pisharody (12)
Beaumont School, St Albans

Burnt Brownies

Haiku poetry

Between you and me
The brownies taste really weird
Maybe there is salt?

I think that you have
Not followed the recipe
And you burnt them all.

Next time please ask me
On how to work the oven
You really messed up.

Estella Reid (12)
Beaumont School, St Albans

In Nature's Grand Theatre

In Nature's Grand Theatre,
Hills adorned in greens and gold,
Seas young yet old,
Peaks climbed,
And countries claimed,
Scream a silent plea,
The moral of this poem,
Hidden yet clear.
Stick to one step; another will appear.
I hope you'll be part of
Nature's Grand Theatre,
Because the upcoming years could become
An unforgivable winter.

Berenika Arciszewska (13)
Blessed Thomas Holford Catholic College, Altrincham

Grief

The five stages of grief, we all experience them one day
Whether it's a relative, close friend
Or something you lose inside you
Either way, it is a loss, one we recover from by
Counting
Counting
Counting
Counting down
Denial is the beginning of our journey, the silence we possess when no words are able to be voiced
Soon followed by the bellowing of anger
Which then morphs into the bargaining chip we make with ourselves to feel even the slightest bit of happiness
This is soon opposed by the depression that seeps in and tints every memory not so rose gold
Numb
Numb
Everything feels numb, until you remember to count
Just count
Only one left
Only one step left until
The end... of pain
This end we call acceptance
The light
That beacon of hope that flourishes
And grows into happiness

That very happiness that reforms us into a new, different person
All is well, feelings start to slowly drift back
Only to be snatched away with that familiar sound of counting
The counting that never really stopped
1, 2, 3, 4, 5
2, 3, 4, 5
3, 4, 5
4, 5
4
4
4
The 4 stays and refuses to leave
It pushes the now haunted memories forward rather than
Shining light on the good ones, the warm ones, the comforting ones
The counting never stops
Sometimes it counts up
But there is the occasional decrease
Until there is only repeat
Repeat of the denial
Repeat of the anger
Repeat of the bargaining
Repeat of the depression
But no acceptance
Acceptance only shows slightly in-between

The counting
Only to disappear and not to be seen
Until the counting begins to sound again
The process repeats itself
With not only the old grief but the newly introduced baggage
That same baggage that is arguably cured with counting
Counting
Counting
Counting
The same counting we live by
Waste time on
Depend on.

Freya Foster (15)
Braeside School, Buckhurst Hill

The Ancient Guardian, Mother Nature

Etched into my core, the solitary beauty of Mother Nature and her everlasting flourishment
That is her time-ticking lore
Sheer blessings she has given us countless times along with her unwavering encouragement
An immemorial guardian who we have let down
Rendered as defenceless as a lifeless *Baum*
Encouragement to achieve ceasing the terrorisation of the calamity humanity is causing
Days slowly draw nature more helpless by the second, its stoicism sapped dry
Its loyal creatures of the land, extinctions creeping closer, a stand-still, a pause
Yet this tragedy swept under the carpet, I ask myself, why, oh why?
A heavenly essence of wildlife put to execution without reason or say
Its inhabitants dying off or taken hostage in zoos whisked all away
Is this worth slaughtering an ancient kingdom for our benefit?
Do you think this is a game?
Because I'm counting down the days that humanity lives up to its name.

Elysia Miller (12)
Braeside School, Buckhurst Hill

A Library Filled With Love

In a dream once, I visited the heavens,
Walked through the gates guarded by angels,
Protecting me from all that was painful,

God handed me these letters, of which I never knew,
He stared at me and said, "They're all about you?"

He handed me the stack of crinkled papers,
Written in all sorts of ways,
Some were just a passing thought,
"In my persisting darkness, her sunshine stays."

He said, "I'll give you a moment."
The gates suddenly closed,
I kept reading,
"I saw the most beautiful girl today,
I hope she sees her beauty,
Hope she truly knows."

I read through every letter,
One about my favourite song, a song that keeps on playing,
The same couple of chords,
Like a church symphonically praying,

The words drift off the paper,
They fall into the air,
And just for a moment,
It feels as if, I'm really there,

The Beautiful Truth - The Hope Of Tomorrow

He learned to play instruments,
Poured his feelings into music because he couldn't gather his words,
He played his love in tunes and sounds,
Because the time to have a conversation was never found,

I never knew?

"What?" God said,

Well, that any of this was true?

You write about your love in the same way people think about you,
A stranger on the pavement.
Your childhood best friend.
All noticed your presence enough to have it penned
In ink,
In thought,
In action,
In word, they all felt that their heart must have heard,

You're not alone in this,

But this is heaven, no?

No, my darling child, this is where your own love must go,
And he wipes the tears from my face,
And kisses my forehead goodbye,

When you meet me in the future,
I'll love you with a library filled,
With every reason why.

Angel Fearon (14)
Braeside School, Buckhurst Hill

Ten Days, One New Life

Ten days left, everything feels different
Nine tiny outfits, ready for someone new
Eight bottles lined up waiting for late nights
Seven blankets, soft as clouds
Six toys waiting to be explored
Five soon-to-be family members
Holding their breath for what's coming
Four books stacked for storytime
Three deep breaths
Two hearts beat in unison
One last night, calm and still
And tomorrow brings a life to fill

Day one: he arrives, his presence makes the world rejoice
Day two: his eyes open, curious and new
Day three: fingers curl around mine
Day four: we learn his soft breath
Day five: the house feels fuller now
Day six: we adjust, slowly, learning day by day
Day seven: every look still surprises us
Day eight: a new routine takes shape
Day nine: we watch him sleep, in awe
Day ten: it's like he's always been here
As if he was the missing piece we needed.

Zaynab Khan (15)
Braeside School, Buckhurst Hill

The Shadow On The Streets Of London

One
A fog emerges from the street
Thick with fear that holds the air
The unknown figure moves through it like a shadow
Hushed and unseen
Two
The moon glistens off its deathly eyes
They are a hallow stare
You freeze beneath its chilling glare
It speaks no words, no sound, it's mute
Three
It owns these streets of London
It's just a game to it
Another night, another body
Another story to unravel
Four
The blade catches the moonlight
Its steel still smeared from its last encounter
No hesitation, it doesn't hold back
Counting, one, two, three, four...
Five
Each scream fades so quickly
Consumed by the empty alleys
It doesn't count the lives
Only the moments
Each beat of a dying heart

Each breath as it slowly fades
Like clocks counting down into oblivion
Six
The streets are smeared with whispers
London fears before them
Yet still, it stalks these London streets
Hungry, desiring more
Seven
No face to remember
Just posters with question marks
The only evidence is the count
And the blood that covers London's streets
Eight
The world longing for him to be captured
It steps to falter
But it moves like time itself
Impossible to catch
Nine
The fog thickens
Swallowing him whole
It aids him, it hides him
And thus, the count
The game continues
Ten
Who knows what wall
Cloaks him from its prey
No matter

The next victim is marked
The waiting ends
You have been chosen
And as it starts to grin
It counts back down to one again.

Alexa Stead (15)
Braeside School, Buckhurst Hill

Blood Spills

The war is in the east
But there is blood in the west
Broken bodies washed up on shores
Blood spilling from their gashes
Spelling words they died for

In the houses of tomorrow
Blood on the ceilings, blood on the walls
Blood on the windows, blood on the floors
Blood spills whilst you selfishly tower
Because you choose to preach hate in exchange for power

Just like your mind, your hands are stained
You try to clean the blood off
But know that it will never wash away
Scrub your hands but blood spills from kitchen tops
Because even the Thames is a river of wrath

Blood spills from your hands
And you smear it on newspapers
The media, puppets of you
Because they are a reflection of your view

Blood spills from your lips
Feeding lies as banquets
To your starving population
Blood spills as people talk
Smearing blood around the whole nation.

Amaya Uddin (15)
Braeside School, Buckhurst Hill

Wishing Your Life Away

Just make it to Friday
I will be happy when it is Friday
Four days till Friday
Three days till Friday
Two days till Friday
One day till Friday
It's Friday, I can't wait till Saturday.

My package is coming in five days
I can't wait till it comes.

In one year I will leave school
I hate school.

The day goes on and we all watch the hours go slowly by, all of us are watching the dark hands of our enemy, time.
Ticking in slow motion.

Exams are soon and can I do it?
How much revision do I need to do to get through it?

Months to weeks, weeks to days, days to hours and hours to minutes
I'm watching the clock again.

It will be Friday soon
It *will* be Friday soon
Friday.

Why wish your life away?
Imagine sunsets on beaches, where you are watching this big yellow yolk melt into the depths of the diamond ocean
You watch the ocean glisten as you hear seagulls squawking and waves crashing
You feel the cold crisp water brush solemnly against your tired leg, the air tastes salty and fresh
You are happy, you are calm, you are at peace.

But what if this happens on a Tuesday, and you were wishing it was Friday
You missed the diamond ocean, the melting sky and the salty sea air
All because you were wishing your life away.

So why *do* we wish our life away?
Why can't we simply just live?

Dilly Roth (15)
Braeside School, Buckhurst Hill

The Stress Of The Test

One more, just one more test, 83%
As the seconds pass, 86%
I await when I can rest, 21%
After the tests, results come, 96%
I look down at them, 99%
Trying to count up the sum, 98%
My heart beating fast, 97%
As the results come back, 99%
How long is this going to last? 82%
Slowly and slowly, the teachers approach me, 99%
When the paper sets down on the table, 99%
I am finally able to see, 99%
What the score on the paper will be, 99%
I look at the paper and count up the points, 93%
One, two, three, four, 87%
It feels like I have frozen my joints, 95%
How come a mark on a paper controls our life? 25%
I sat there thinking, 20%
Some results hit like a knife, 82%
While some sit there in relief, sinking, 21%
But there is something else, 92%
One more, just one more result, 99%

One more result is awaited to come, 98%
I think I got them correct, 54%
At least some, 97%
Seconds pass, 98%
Lessons go by, 99%
The time has come at last, 99%
The result has come, 99%
I checked the score, 98%
I worked out the sum, 97%
And I am in my long-awaited rest, 20%
Finally, no more, no more tests, 0%.

Afaaf Faraz (13)
Braeside School, Buckhurst Hill

Adulthood

When you are young, life is light and free
Like golden leaves on a sunlit tree
Climbing high with untamed delight
The world is vast, the future is bright!

In those days, we played hide-and-seek
Built Lego towers that touched the skies and peaked
No worries clouded our minds
Just laughter and joy in the games we'd find

But as you grow, the winds begin to shift
Skies once clear now foggy, a drift
What was simple turns to complicated and strange
Childhood magic replaced, by life's change

Alarms, deadlines and bills to pay
Responsibilities piling on every day
Work takes over, the fun starts to fade
The games we played are now memories that we made

Every now and then, I catch a spark
A glimpse of my younger self in the dark
I look back fondly on carefree days
On fearless climbs and endless plays

Forwards I stride, unafraid of the storm
For within me a fire still keeps me warm
The future calls, a path unknown
And I will face it all, fully *grown*.

Siya Grewal Badesha (12)
Braeside School, Buckhurst Hill

Loop

One, two, three - I start the day,
A painted smile, I'm on display.
Four, five, six, pretend it's fine,
A laugh, a joke, I toe the line.

Seven, eight, nine - it's all the same,
Routines just blur, they have no name.
I spin in circles, lose my ground,
Each day's a loop that pulls me down.

Ten, eleven, twelve - the mask stays tight,
But inside feels like an endless night.
Thirteen, fourteen - I can't feel,
I wonder if this numbness is real.

Fifteen, sixteen, seventeen -
I play the part, the perfect scene.
Eighteen, nineteen - keep it light,
Hold back the dark with all my might.

Twenty, twenty-one, then back to one,
The loop restarts, my act's not done.
Counting days, I keep the score,
But I don't want to count any more.

So I'll smile wide, pretend to care,
Laugh loud enough to hide despair.
But underneath, I wish they'd see,
The endless loop that's swallowing me.

Eliza Muneer (16)
Braeside School, Buckhurst Hill

Behind The Mask

Behind the mask, whispers crawl,
Stories hidden, forgotten by all.
A face you see, calm and still,
But beneath, there's more - an untold thrill.

Eyes that glimmer but never speak,
Conceal the mysteries they seek.
The mask is quiet, a perfect disguise,
But behind it flickers a thousand lies.

Shadows twist in the unseen space,
Guarding secrets time can't erase.
Each layer hides a deeper truth,
Lost in the echoes of ancient youth.

Behind the mask, the world is grey,
A silent dance, night and day.
What lies beneath - no one can know,
A hidden path where few will go.

Perhaps the mask will never fall,
Perhaps it guards the greatest of all.
A mystery locked, a story sealed -
Behind the mask, nothing is revealed.

Aiza Iftikhar (12)
Braeside School, Buckhurst Hill

Factors Of The Royal Albert Hall!

Five percent of the time, you're thinking of all the work you've put in.
Ten percent of the time, you're rehearsing the words and your patience is thin.
Five percent of the time, you're counting down the hours.
Ten percent of the time, you feel you are special, that you've got the power.
Five percent of the time, you're overwhelmed with pride and happiness that you've made it this far.
You were scared to open the door to new things, but now you're glad that you'd left it ajar.
Most things take courage, so you know you must give it your all...
The rest of the time? I am just happy I went to the Albert Hall!

Matilda-Rose Akeru (11)
Braeside School, Buckhurst Hill

Stage Fright

1... 2... 3... 4
My heart beating out of my chest, stress filling my brain.
5... 6... 7... 8
Lights covering the stage.
9... 10... 11... 12
Commotion of dancers remembering steps backstage.
13... 14... 15... 16
Going through choreography in my mind.
17... 18... 19... 20
Watching the dancers on stage going carefully through the dance.
21... 22... 23... 24
Music starting to slow.
25... 26... 27... 28
Performers exiting the stage.
29... 30... 31... 32
Lights dimming.
33
Audience applauding.
34
The first group entering.
35
Music beginning.
36
First step on stage.

37
In my starting position.
38
Listening to the beats.
39
First group starting.
40!
I begin.

Beatrice Neighbour (15)
Braeside School, Buckhurst Hill

Puzzle Of Life

The first puzzle is easy
Only a few pieces
All we do is eat, sleep, play, repeat.

The second puzzle is okay
A bit harder
We have to start learning and stop playing.

The third puzzle is getting harder
More learning
We go to school
We do exams and study nearly every day.

The fourth puzzle, it's a struggle
Harder exams and more studying, so boring
There are too many pieces
It's too stressful.

The fifth puzzle, it stresses me out
I do it wrong
I do it right
I can't sleep at night
What if I can't do something?
I don't want to get fired.

The sixth puzzle is the last puzzle to solve
No more stress
No more learning
Now we are free!

Imaan Mir (12)
Braeside School, Buckhurst Hill

The Rain Cries With You

When you're all alone, just remember
The rain cries with you.
When you're fighting through difficulties and
All you can do is cry,
The rain cries with you.

The rain has been there waiting
For you to notice him,
When he saw you in a corner
Holding your emotion,
He burst out crying for you.

Yet you chose to conceal them,
In those few moments
The rain that helped you,
Cared for you, loved you,
He felt like you abandoned them.

The more you ignored them,
The more he saw your tragic state.
The more you ignored them,
The deeper into your thoughts you sank.

Yumnah Khan (14)
Braeside School, Buckhurst Hill

Death's Door

We've always knocked on death's door
But no one ever answers
Even as a kid
From the moment you are born
Till the day you die
As a baby, you learn to walk
As a kid, you go to school and count down till you get home
When you are a teen, you start counting to death
Even when you don't want to
There is a countdown till you die but you can't see it
When you are older you reflect on your childhood
Wishing you were still there
You couldn't wait until you were grown
You always count the major milestones, even death
Counting, counting, counting, till death finally answers the door.

Lilly Kenee (13)
Braeside School, Buckhurst Hill

The Bullying Poem

You may think you're cool 'cause you call me names
You may think I'm hurting on the inside
You may even choose to do something horrible
But do you think I'm just going to run and hide?

Lots of people look to you scared
And if they are not you will turn on your rage
But when you speak to them they will just cower.

People obeying your every demand
But if someone bigger came along
You would just run away in fear
You're not just a bully you're a coward.

Shreeya Mehta (11)
Braeside School, Buckhurst Hill

Showjumping

Horse riding is a sport
Like a battle with no talk
No violence, no noise
The next step is HOYS
You can feel the audience staring at you
Your butterflies rushing through
1. Your horse tenses
2. Your canter commences
3. You take off and you fly
4. As you come to the last jump, you let out a long and relieved sigh
5. And then you fly for the last time.

Sadie King (11)
Braeside School, Buckhurst Hill

To Summon A Truth

Something along the lines of my mother,
I suppose.
The heartbeat that bore mine
beating against the other as my tiny hands
gripped hers.
Lessons on courage and respect
forming the woman I am becoming.

Her truth summons mine
a promise to be there
and support me
in the shape of lemon and honey when I'm ill
and long hugs when sadness overcomes me.
Bringing me up with the love every child deserves
through battles of her own
she heals wounds she did not make
and wipes tears that did not drop from her eyes.

If I should have a daughter,
I hope my truth summons hers
like calling to like
with stories before bed
and later on
clothes to borrow for a night out.
I hope her heart beats as strongly
for her mother

as my heart beats
for mine.
Paving the way through the trials of adolescence
until she takes flight
to summon a truth of her own.

Josie Richards (17)
Brighton Hove & Sussex Sixth Form College, Hove

The Beautiful Truth

In a world where our sins lie at the heart of our soul,
I gained life and honesty with the sunrise.
So that when the day comes, I can achieve my goal.
I grew as I waited with hope and maybe sometimes with despair,
For a chance to hear the words of truth on show.
I waited and watched repeatedly the sun rise,
And once the sunset came,
My eyes fluttered closed and my mouth sealed,
In hopes to have my soul finally healed.
But when I opened my eyes on the other side,
I'm asked to speak of a beautiful truth.
And so, when my soundless words are echoed back to me,
My feelings are left in no place, no time.
With only my name engraved in stone,
For those who had once loved me,
To call out for.

Samin Toofan (17)
Brighton Hove & Sussex Sixth Form College, Hove

A Life Built On Lies

When we were younger, our greatest dilemma
Was whether our lunch came on the blue or red plate,
When Christmas was full of magic, the joy didn't feel fake.
Overwhelming work didn't drown and drag us down,
Finger-painted pictures littered the ground.
Lies were only told to keep those dimpled smiles on our faces,
We never had to worry about words that seemed out of place.
Tooth Fairy, Santa Claus, Easter bunny too,
Everything was perfect, I suppose it was too good.
We traded the easy smiles and childish giggles,
For mascara stains and drooping luggage under our eyes.
Emotional baggage, so many achy hearts,
Please take us all back to the start.
Please, won't you please heal our broken hearts?
Shackled minds,
Led to believe money cures all aches, seen and unseen, but it doesn't.
Those perfect teeth and liquid-filled cheeks don't make you happy,
Life's still bleak, no one's perfect.
Perfection's a lie,
Sold by the brands with their names in the sky.
One day I'll go up, I'll be there too,
Free from the chains of a world of lies.

Taylia Edy (17)
Brockenhurst College, Brockenhurst

Chains

They tell us we're quiet and sweet
Born to raise, to keep our homes in line
But we're more than the roles forced to repeat
We are strong and we've got power by design

They say we're just a prize for a man to claim
A body to shape, a heart to hurt, lost dreams to confine
But we aren't for sale in this crooked game.
We're not your dolls, nor your tools to refine

They teach us to shrink and smile through our pain
To play soft and follow his lead,
But we're done being shackled by a man's chain
Our voices shall rise, we will never concede

We'll rewrite rules and take back our right
We're wild, we're fierce, we are who we are meant to be
We'll tear down walls and set men's world alight
We're women, we're free.

Clobha Moffat (16)
Brockenhurst College, Brockenhurst

Wolf In Sheep's Clothing

I am a wolf swallowed by sheep's clothing,
shambling through life like a three-legged lamb.

I am a wolf suffocated by sheep's clothing,
"What if's?" and "Who am I's?" running through my hands
like a waterfall of regret.

I am a wolf trapped in sheep's clothing,
expectations and pressure weighing me down like wads of
wool upon my shoulders.

I am not a sheep, just a wolf in sheep's clothing,
embraced by the warmth like it's my mother and my
siblings.

I am a wolf, I like bugs and mud and the sky when it's
raining.
I am not a sheep, I don't like sunsets, roses, make-up or
dresses.

I am a wolf, even if I'm the only one who notices.

I am a wolf.

Atlas Pollock (16)
Brockenhurst College, Brockenhurst

Colour

The wall in my bedroom
It hasn't been painted
Since I was a child
The paint cracks.

A spill of colours
Emerges from the crack
Pouring into the world
Filling the room with life.

The crack widens with age
More happiness spilling out
I take it for granted
My room is already so bright.

The crack seals slowly
I don't notice at first
But soon the room gets duller
Something is missing.

I find it sealed
And take a hammer
Crack it open.
Nothing but bricks.

Taylor Barnes (16)
Brockenhurst College, Brockenhurst

The Consequence Of Too Many Thoughts

Have you heard of the old man
Who's enlightenment stuns all around?
He just woke up one day
With the most profound things to say
In his words, the real truth was found.

These truths he would always confide
In the nearest soul, who never knew why
One night, he woke up his wife
To tell the love of his life
That lobsters probably think fish can fly.

Emerson Poole (17)
Brockenhurst College, Brockenhurst

My Hopes For You

I hold myself high,
But I'm really high.
My mind is something I want to hide,
The only place where both good and evil breathe.

Sitting on a fragile line,
Where my mind holds zero lies.
From nothing to something,
Yet fate is unknown.
Will I cry today or tomorrow?
Learning that it's okay to be,
Even if I am nothing - you are not.

I only crave your happiness,
To how far you can go.
Hopefully, I helped reach your goals,
Even when the day is over.
All I want is for you to remember,
No matter how dark it seems,
The sun will come true.

Jessica-Louise Adams (14)
Chilton Bridge School, Chilton Cantelo

What Makes Me, Me?

Behind locked eyes
I sit and observe
The colours of my youth
Only from there I can see
What makes me, me
My so-called, 'Beautiful Truth'

I'm drawn to the passion of summer
As crimson lays the ground for our feet
Yet my summer's face
Longs for the warm embrace
Of wistful winter heat

Hazy days of woollen jumpers
Melt into soulful nights
And through this tender terracotta haze
Shines a charming moonlit light

In the depths of autumn
Where the nights become twice as cold
The coffee is twice as hot
I ruminate the secluded peace
To untie my inner knots

So what makes me, me?
I ask myself on one of these autumnal nights
Is it the actions I take that culminate
Into their perception of wrong or right?

We constantly evolve and develop and grow
But is this an internal revelation
For others may see a version of me
Displaying passion, anguish or elation

The colours of my life are what make me, me
My passions, my experiences, my dreams
I apply each colour to my inner canvas
To paint a portrait of who I see

Some brushstrokes may be forgotten
Or painted over and over again
Each time a melody emerges from my guitar
Yet another layer of colour is attained

But what makes me, me
May not make you, you
We may not share the same perspective
On the music that fills my headphones
Or the art I produce
For it is all purely subjective

As it takes a life to learn to love
It takes a life to learn yourself
But it's up to you to seek out your 'Beautiful Truth'
So let it blossom and reveal itself.

Oliver Spenser-Morris (16)
Culford School, Culford

The Pit

We gorge ourselves on red meat and red wine.
My god! We crave it so desperately, don't we?
We crave to be full-
To be fulfilled. Proud
Of our satisfactory systematic, white-picket lives,
Order,
Order!
(Hidden behind is a chaos, spasming around a pitiful nothing)

We want to be full! Full of produce, never ceasing to consume,
We want to be full! Full of merry and joy! One bottle, two bottles, three? four?
What are we but bottomless pits? Consuming our way to a mass-produced grave.
Gravestone carved by machines, flowers cut by underpaid, underfed, yet not unloved hands.

Are you satisfied?
What would you rate your satisfaction on a scale of one to ten?
One!

The bottomless pit that drags your loneliness ever deeper, festering and feral,
Clawing gripping grappling, frantically searching for something -
No - Someone! to hold onto.

The wet-slick, flesh-fussy, pulsating walls of the consuming pit crave most desperately: meat and wine, yes.
But also, the gentle, bittersweet disposition of a painfully human comrade, vulnerable in their cell of desire.

Alistair Walker
Esher College, Thames Ditton

Disguised As Society

Disguised as society
Within all the trends
Is a woman, kind and caring
For her sight is unique
Different and fun
For her hair is colourful, lively
Yet her eyes are grey
Drained
As the colour has faded
From society
You and I
The grey that fills her eyes
Building the tension to fit it
Then to look back and think
"How boring"
For we are women in society
Yet we are never enough.

Isabel Cooke (13)
Hans Price Academy, Weston-Super-Mare

Betrayed

Every day, where the sun won't shine,
I wonder to myself at school -
Who should I talk to?
People pass me and whisper to each other,
Giggling to themselves,
Sometimes I feel like I'm the one left out.
I try to make friends, they betray me after a week -
What's even the point of me trying?
There's no hope, no glimpse of escape, I'm trapped,
I can't escape, escape from everyone.
It explains why I'm dull, stubborn -
No one can accept me.
I try to make friends with others,
They already have friends so I'm the odd one out.
I try to isolate myself from others but I can't,
The urge to talk to others is consuming me.
I cry, I beg for the world to stop treating me like this -
But why can't I just be normal
And have friends like other people?
I want to be normal...
I had a friend once, she was close friends with me
But then she had to move away.

I felt helpless
And when she came to visit my school for a day,
She didn't even notice me
And that's when I felt utterly and hopelessly betrayed.

Valentina Ciechanowska (13)
Higham Lane School, Nuneaton

The Beautiful Truth Of September

I was feeling it deep,
As change was coming, coming next week.

With science labs and PE halls,
With sports events and fancy balls,
With locker rooms with shiny floors,
And dance studios and so much more.

With the opportunities,
With the positivities.
With the joy of new friends,
And loads of new trends.

Whilst the rooms might not be presidential,
They will still most likely be exciting residentials.
With the endless choices of thrilling activities,
And overcoming all your sensitivities.

The intimidating walls will become opportunity calls,
The word cages will complete our knowledge pages.
Although the transition might not be gentle,
I will make some new friends and it will be monumental.

Oh, and I was feeling it deep, really deep,
As change was coming, coming this week!

Aariya Kaur Bassi (11)
King Edward VI High School For Girls, Birmingham

The Beautiful Truth

My heart and soul
is what makes me whole.
Inside of me
is making history.
Open up my heart
tear me apart
and find deep within
me - outside and in.

Explore my depths; see my dream
watch the components of my personality team.
Separate them; dissect me
watch how in my mind I am set free.
Take reading - my long-lost friend
our love for each other shall never end.
I love a story coming to life in my mind
and how it is my imagination you must find.

We are all living anomalies
we are all different, unique and shall be.
The different hobbies that create myself
like the variety of books on the shelf.
My beautiful truth - what a wonderful thing!
Made of archery, reading, writing and swimming.
I am my own person - of that I'm content
as everyone else must begin their own ascent.

Serena Santra (11)
King Edward VI High School For Girls, Birmingham

Books

The roaring blizzard out the window
And pine scent of burning logs
Brings the warmth of winter to me

As I read, reality blurs
No more blizzard, no more pine scent
Only the story that I read
Is in my head, forever speaking

Shall I read of damsels in distress
Or read of monsters in the night?
Of childhood fantasies or teenage dreams of love?

As night falls and the story ends
I feel my eyelids drooping shut
As I slumber in my bed
Adventures await me in my head.

Melinda King (12)
Langholm Academy, Langholm

The Children Of The Compass

Early Esther and Eager Earl, the children of the east,
Weary Wendy and Wandering Wallace, the children of the west,
Naive Nora and Nice Nixon, the children of the north,
Lethargic Lisa and Lonely Lucas, the children of the left,
Yes, you may have thought south, but no, the writer of this poem appears to be great at writing, but *terrible* at directions,
The east is elegant,
The west is wise,
The north is neat,
And the left is despised!
They all get along, or at least we hope,
And when left rules the world, I hope they will cope!

Cara Green (12)
Lochgilphead High School, Lochgilphead

Me

L ast time I felt truly free
I s when I went to Manchester with school
A nd there were no parents to tell us off.
R ight before we were leaving, someone broke something
A nd the teachers made his parents pay.

T he real me is someone who loves to read
H owever, not many people I know know that.
O ne memory that still haunts me is when
M y baby brother was born but he needed
A nurse to take him somewhere to help him.
S ome people know this but only my most trusted friends know.

Liara Thomas-Lewis (11)
Ludlow CE School, Ludlow

Struggles

Whenever I go somewhere new,
I find it hard to fit in with the crew,
As I don't know how people stick like glue.

It's my weakness, and sadly that will be,
As I can never be like the others.
I don't know if people face it or if it's only me.

Every time I try to sign up for the team,
Everyone looks at me, muttering to themselves,
As I always get rejected. Oh, why me?

All the time, I struggle with facing my fears,
I always look like the odd one out.
Every week, every month and every year.

But one day, I might change.
I might be famous.
Oh, I might be on the stage.

I just hope that happens
And doesn't get ripped like wrappers,
As it will be a disaster.

Sameera Ahamed (12)
Manchester Islamic Grammar School For Girls, Chorlton

Challenges

We all go through challenges no matter what they are,
some can be as big as a mountain and some can be small,
it's important to realise that you're never the only one,
as every person on this planet goes through it all,
those moments are called challenges,
that's part of being a human,
and that's called life, after all.

If you want to become what you desire to be,
you have to conquer the challenges,
master the skills you need to learn.

This is a poem about my own experience,
the fear I faced when I started a new phase,
moving from primary to high school
everything was about to change,
building a feeling of fear inside me,
that's the challenge I had to face.
Everything was new and so strange
I gathered my courage and wanted no fear,
I learned to adjust and freed myself from this chain,
step by step, I started to push myself,
believing in my abilities, when I expressed myself.
I made new friends and gave a public speech,
even though lots of people were staring at me.
It made me happy and I felt so proud,
the challenges I faced are over now.

Let me share a secret with you,
you can overcome your challenges too,
all you have to do is remember this,
as scary as it may seem to be,
by being brave and trying new things,
challenging it might be,
but you will succeed.

Zaynab Ijaz (11)
Manchester Islamic Grammar School For Girls, Chorlton

Struggles

Overwhelming me, day by day,
Trying to deal with the struggles my way.
How do I cope? More and more,
Things add to my list, an ever-growing chore.

Some things easy, some things hard,
Others quick, others dragging, leaving me scarred,
When will I ever be free?
I'm sore from these overwhelming struggles, why me?

Why? When will I be free?
I can't deny my head is spinning,
A hurricane of jobs, each task screaming,
Demanding to be checked off, then forgotten and lost.

Unless...
A guiding light, illuminating my life,
Putting my stress away, slicing through strife.
Can I escape? Is there peace in sight?
Or will I drown in this endless fight?

Fatima Chaudhary (13)
Manchester Islamic Grammar School For Girls, Chorlton

Identity

Some people are white
Some people are black
Some people are both!
Some people are none.

Some people are gay!
Or bi, or pan, or straight
Some people like to eat
Some people worry about weight.

All people have hopes
All people have dreams
All people have fears
Or something in-between.

All people believe in something
Even if it's nothing at all
All people are similar
Even if some are big
And some are small.

Some people have blue eyes
Some have brown or green
Some people have a mix of two
Or five, or six, or three!

Some people have scars
Some people have smooth skin
But what we are on the outside
Doesn't define us within.

All people have likes
All people have dislikes
All people struggle and feel
Some act as if emotions
Are not even real.

Love yourself today
And forever!

Ava Sapani (12)
Mount House School, Hadley Wood

The Truth

What have we done?
The stylish clothes we buy,
It may seem fun,
But have you seen the people cry?

What have we done?
Thousands of litres of water, lost for a single garment,
Lakes dried up as if never existing, gone,
Even you should lament.

What have we done?
Imagine the factory looming over you,
As you turn the corrupted run,
Leaving nothing but unkept promises and trauma, too.

What have we done?
All for greed,
The people abused,
Us with our fast fashion,
The people with their low wage.

Who does the fault belong to?
The big companies, or us?
And that is the truth.

Alicia Delacour (13)
Newlands Girls' School, Maidenhead

The Truth About Chickens

Chickens live a happy life,
Living peacefully with their wife,
Until we come along and put them in a cage,
Then we watch them peck our grain in rage,
We stalk them peacefully, then stab with a knife,
Now it's in the afterlife,
They are tasty, tasty birds,
With no chicks to make any herds,
We sprinkle herbs upon their legs,
Then into the oven, it goes without a beg,
Till they are crispy and yummy,
With just enough fat to go in our tummy,
So next time when you lick your lips,
Think about those chickens on the warships.

Eleanor Franzen (12)
Newlands Girls' School, Maidenhead

Truth And Trust

Truth like life is a beautiful thing,
It should be treated as the precious treasure it is.
Truth like trust is hard to earn,
But the best thing is that it helps us learn.
Learn to try our best not to lie,
Learn to become more truthful people.
Trust we gain by telling the truth,
But it is up to us to make that move.
Truth is made of a beautiful thing,
It is the stuff that holds friendships and families together.
It will win, deceit will fail,
The truth will always prevail.

Holly Tooley (11)
Newlands Girls' School, Maidenhead

The Willow Tree

Down by the hollows, by the trickling stream,
Lies an old, lean willow tree,
With a swish and a sway, as free as can be.

While a group of children dance with glee,
Around the willow tree, seasons pass with an
Orange leaf, to snow so white and a summer's breeze.

Down by the hollows, by the trickling stream,
Lies a group of children, grown and free.

Frida Macfarlane (11)
Notre Dame Senior School, Cobham

Blood On The Ghost

Flowers bloom
Ghosts gloom
Round the clock
Tick tock
Round the red rose
Well, I suppose
Blood on the ghost
Who finds it gross
Out on the coast
We find it the most
Echoes of the blood on the ghost.

Savannah Greene (12)
Notre Dame Senior School, Cobham

The Ocean

How do I tell the ocean that her salt burns as it seeps into my cuts?
She only means to wash away the blood.
How do I tell the ocean my eyes sting with her caresses?
She means only to wipe away my tears.
How do I tell the ocean to stop pushing me back up to the surface?
She means only to save me from the depths of her abode.
Dear Ocean, please stop. I know you mean well, but you've done enough.

Wahi Noor (16)
Royal Latin School, Buckingham

Identity: The Truth That Defines Me

Identity
The truth that defines me

Could be what's in my heart
Or my nationality
Maybe it's where I start
Might be my personality

Possibly my future dreams
Maybe what invokes my tears
To others, it might be how I seem
Some of it could be my fears

Could it be my accomplishments?
Maybe it is my beliefs?
What if it's my competence
My skills and my abilities?

Many things make up identity
But personally, I think it's me.

Matthew Dix (15)
Rutlish School, Merton

The Roots To Be Free

As the doors went round,
I got used to the sound,
Although I felt bound,
To the whirring of the bus.

I stepped out into the air,
Someone's chest was bare,
Which gave me a scare,
But then I got used to it.

The airport was big,
With a curious creature on the floor.
It looked like it was trying to dig
And didn't want to go through the door.

As our number was called,
We went to our gate.
A baby started to bawl,
When they called those who were late.

As we walked up to the plane,
This was anything but tame.
The inside looked like a train
And then we were off!

The Beautiful Truth - The Hope Of Tomorrow

A little wobble,
A little bobble,
And a little hobble,
When we touched down.

And then I was free!

Alexander Harper (12)
Rutlish School, Merton

The Truth Is What People Tell Us

- The truth is only what people tell us
How do we know the world isn't flat?
- People told us so
How do we know colour is objective to all of us?
- People told us so
How do we know we live in a democracy?
- People told us so
Could pain be an illusion?
Could we be in a simulation?
Is this even a poem?
Who would know
Is the truth even achievable?
- ...

(Digital test sample, 42,602) 5th Gen AI

Deleted.

Toni Bosch-Garcia (13)
Rutlish School, Merton

What Is The Meaning Of Truth?

A fact, or principle, that is thought to be true by most people.
It would seem to be general truth that nothing is as straightforward as it first seems.
The entire system of belief is based on a few simple truths.
The truth does not harm.

Nickson Wamala (12)
Rutlish School, Merton

The Beautiful World

Tempora mutantur, seasons sway in the glamorous dance of time
Rivers flow gently as mountains stand tall
The sun kissed and blessed when this wonderful journey began.

Fields of gold where wildflowers bloom
Whispers of nature dispel a gloom
A symphony plays while the forest breathes
Deep with rustling leaves and the deepest heartbeat.

Oceans weave a tapestry both fierce and strong
Stars stroke the sky with shimmering light
Guiding lost wanderers through the velvet night.

In every beam, life unfolds like a delicate dream
From the tiniest seed to the grandest tree
Each moment a treasure, each breath a decree.

Tempora mutantur, yet still we find beauty in chaos
Peace intertwined. So let us wander, let our spirits soar
In this beautiful world, forever explore.

George Emmerson (11)
Seaham High School, Seaham

Make A Change

Can you imagine?
A world with just humans?
That wouldn't be right, would it?
No forests filled full of fauna,
That wouldn't be right, would it?
No seas swarming with sealife,
That wouldn't be right, would it?
That's a world we're going to discover
If we don't act now,
So, would you rather we make a change
And let the animals thrive and survive
Or would you like to see,
The animals suffer?
It's not just the animals we'll lose because of deforestation,
It's our sheets of paper as well!
It's not just the sea life we'll lose,
It's the delicious seafood as well!
So to solve these problems, my advice to you is three words:
Make. A. Change.
Please, if you care, stop destroying our planet and do not litter.

Jessica Moon (11)
Seaham High School, Seaham

Meaningful Crystals

The thing I care about the most,
Is special and unique,
It isn't a duck or some toast,
But some special crystals.

Crystals can help your mental health,
They can help protect,
They can help you love yourself,
Even give intelligence.

Let's find out what they mean,
Amethysts can calm you
Lapis lazuli brings understanding
And rose quartz brings love.

Citrine generates positive energy,
Amazonite helps calm the soul,
Carnelian brings creativity,
And apatite symbolises freedom.

All of these crystals are meaningful,
They can calm you,
And protect you,
Crystals are happiness.

Lauren Blagden
Seaham High School, Seaham

Souls

N ever in my life have I seen a sane soul
O thers are just selfish souls.

S ouls are what make a person whole
O thers are silly souls
U nder no circumstances have I seen a soul with sense
L ovely souls can still be senseless souls
S ouls can be what they want to be.

F ull of sense souls might not be silly or sane
O thers are silent souls
U nder the weather souls are fine, they'll get through it
N o matter how sane, silent, senseless, silly or selfish you are, it
D oesn't matter, you are a soul.

Megan Westwood (11)
Seaham High School, Seaham

The Mask Of My Mind

The mask of my mind, sweet yet evil,
A cover for my 'bad' emotions,
A smile scours my face but, in reality, I'm crying on the inside,
A double life I live,
Joyous and happy, anxious and depressed,
A bottle sits in my mind,
Where you can find my locked-up pride,
Look even further and you'll see,
The built-up rage inside of me,
I fail to feel much glee,
But maybe it's just me,
Maybe it's just anxiety having a grip on me,
Whatever it may be,
I wish it could let go of me,
The mask of my mind,
Who knows when it will leave.

Lilly-Anne Laing (11)
Seaham High School, Seaham

Believe In Yourself

The world is full of truth,
The world is full of lies,
But the truths sometimes lie,
And the lies tell the truth,

So the answer?
Don't trust, don't believe,
Just be there.

Don't change, just exist,
Just be there. Or
Be the one to find the truth,
To tell the truth,
To be the light in the dark,

You can do that,
You have done that,
By being you.

Matthew Saville (11)
Seaham High School, Seaham

Imperfections

In a world where mirrors show our flaws,
We chase perfection, break our own laws,
The weight of judgement hangs in the air,
Every glance a whisper, every look a stare.

Masks of confidence, where hearts feel the strain,
A race for approval, drowned in the rain,
We curate our lives through a digital lens,
Yet behind the fluorescent screens, the silence descends.

Fear of imperfections, the void of the soul,
We seek validation to fill up the hole,
In crowded rooms, we still feel alone,
Yearning for a connection, but tethered to stone.

Insecurity hums like a low distant song,
It tells us we're weak, it tells us we're wrong,
Beneath all the surface, the cracks and the scars,
Stories of strength, like the light from the stars.

So, let's dare to be real, to stumble, trip and fall,
Embrace our imperfections, stand proud and tall,
For in vulnerability, we find a common ground,
Life is short, don't care what people think
That's where true strength is found.

Amisha Naurang (15)
St Bees School, St Bees

The Beautiful Truth

A lie is a creature that eats you alive
Pain and suffering lurking inside
A plethora of screams explode from your mouth
You hold in the truth, but it can only come out
Like Poe's tattletale heart on the wall
Floating over an abyss about to fall
Your heart is chained with the deeds you've done
Not telling the truth and flying too close to the sun
All of a sudden, the burden is lifted
After telling the truth you have been gifted
The beautiful feeling swimming through your mind
Leaving lies and dishonesty behind.

Alice Gould (11)
St Bees School, St Bees

The Beautiful Truth

The beautiful truth is you.

I utterly despise the way you take over my thoughts,
My mind,
My beliefs,
I utterly despise the way you make me see you
As the truth.
As *my* truth.

You portray yourself as my god, as my only way of thinking,
As my only possible option.

You make me want to let your jagged teeth sink into my soft skin,
Let you crack open my brittle bones to reveal the sweet marrow within each one.

I utterly despise the way you make me miss you,
After I've willed you away
Begged for you to get out of my head.

But my beautiful truth is you.

After you lead me through your endless maze of criticisms
And insults
And threats.
You unintentionally show me myself,
You show me every little detail,

From the moles and marks and scars,
To the crooked teeth and tired eyes.
It's because of you,
I see myself.
Unguided, unassisted, without you:
I see my own beautiful truth.

Eve McMullan (16)
St Bees School, St Bees

The Beautiful Truth

Man, I love that corporate greed
Although, I doubt those below love the life they lead
Somehow mere stepping stones to see
But to them, I'm unattainable and make-believe
Roll and rein in the bonuses
Run ragged, wreak havoc and increase the onuses
Bring out the gold chains and the flashy cars
Cover up, ignore and fake the battle scars
The CEOs, suited and booted, take all the glory
While I sit, soundless, writing the next algorithm shortly.

Suproto Mansur (17)
St Bees School, St Bees

The Beautiful Truth

These are things that we think about,
Things that you want to be,
Things you want to do
These are things that you *think* you cannot do
Just silly things in my head, you say,
They will never be real, you say,
You need to believe because...
These are our dreams, you can make them happen,
Just close your eyes and see the path life takes you,
Trust me, it is going to be amazing.

Imogen Freeman (12)
St Bees School, St Bees

Unrequited Love

I was there when you needed a shoulder to cry on,
I was the one who comforted you,
At your lowest,
I was the one who hugged and rubbed your back,
Even though I don't like physical touch,
I held your hand,
And kept you close,
When I needed to cry, I held it back for you,
But for me to be pushed into the dark,
When I needed you,
Left alone, to cry over you,
Told to calm down or stop being a wimp,
I was the one who was called the attention seeker,
And as I see, there's no comfort from you,
I see you at school,
You look so happy,
When I'm not with you,
I feel my eyes begin to sweat,
But it's not sweat,
It's tears

Eva Stirling (12)
St Ninian's High School, Kirkintilloch

I Play Rugby

I play rugby
For Lenzie RFC
It's what I like to play
I play as scrum half
Also known as number nine
Make sure you know
It's not a game of size
I play rugby
For Lenzie RFC.

Finlay McMaster (11)
St Ninian's High School, Kirkintilloch

The Thoughts Of People's Minds

I feel that some people are hiding something
Hiding their thoughts deep down, but how will they be helped?
Constantly reminded of what someone is going through,
Also getting that connection with your mind,
There's nothing that can stop that connection,
Feel what's right,
Extend your feelings,
Anything on your mind,
Let it be free and let it be out,
X-ray powers to encounter what one is capable of,
And what is not,
Pray to the one that helps you,
You yourself are a superpower,
Realise that someone could have a condition that isn't visible,
But it's there,
Everyone has a beginning, where is yours?
Don't worry, you have a lot of time,
Sad times for the ones who abuse the power of a beginning,
Sometimes, for whatever reason, let your voice be heard, and proud,
Time to go, but before you do,
Let's calm you down,
Happiness is inside all of us, but a few of us can't see it yet,

Opportunities come by, some may be inside out,
But there's always a route,
Underneath that stubborn face,
Might be someone's forever grace,
Glory of that one thing that we feel great about,
Today is a new day, like tomorrow will be great,
What are you thinking?
Share with us what is in your mind,
Don't rush, you have lots of time,
Enlighten the way your mind talks to you,
It's not what we all do.

Lilly-Mai Unsted (14)
St Philip Howard Catholic High School, Barnham

Blank Canvas

Everyone has a story to tell,
A blank canvas to paint,
A life to make.
Some people have a messy life,
A splattered canvas.
Some people have a neat and tidy life,
A tidy canvas.
Some people have a sad, quiet life,
A grieving life.
I wonder what everyone's canvas is,
Is it in their minds or on paper?
Everyone is different,
With a different life.
A different backstory.
There could be a person in your class
Or at your school
Who's quiet and reserved
Or they could be outgoing
And happy all the time,
But actually,
They could be having a sad,
Worryful, alone life.
But maybe they are just,
Happy and bubbly all the time.

So in life, paint your own picture,
Sing your own song
And just love life in general.

Niah Linard-Salter (11)
St Philip Howard Catholic High School, Barnham

Secondary

Memories made, demonstrative depart
Moderately merry, wanting a splendid start
While wanting wholeness, experienced emptiness
Small somethings lower loneliness

Starting secondary school, sweating speedily
Finding friends, feeling first class
Also worried, and harassed by homework
Craft compression in class

Now new starts seem sociable
Uselessly unhappy, finding resolutions to my regrets
The environment endlessly adapts
But it's in safety because secondary is my being and breath.

Stanley Brown (11)
St Philip Howard Catholic High School, Barnham

Mr Fox

Night falls beyond us
A shadow sweeps through the grass
Leash and dog tight in hand
We stand quietly, unlike a loud band
A curious face appears out of the dark
Leaving no trace or even a mark
Nose twitching
Ears pointing
Beneath the single lamp
There it is
The beautiful glow
Like a blissful kiss
As the wind begins to blow
Gold, luxurious fur glistens in the light
With elegance, he dances oh so bright
Our hearts melt as one
Pushing away any harm done
A graceful tail follows behind him
We stare in awe, not feeling a limb
This is Mr Fox
But we sure feel lots
We slowly approach, our hands like ice
This fox is a pure paradise
We feed him food that we've shown
We feel as if he's one of our own

Although it may not sound like much
But soon enough, we could touch
Dreams and wishes all come true
It couldn't have been done without you
Love in our hearts is sealed with locks
To our one and only, Mr Fox.

Harley Parker (15)
Stantonbury High School, Stantonbury

Wildlife's Song

In the heart of the forest where the tall trees sway
Sunlight shines softly through the leaves
Whispers of the wind echo through the branches
Nature's own chorus, a wild, vibrant murmur.

Mountains stand proudly, dressed in white crowns
Streams laugh and dance, tracing their way down
Wildflowers bloom in a brilliant array of hues
Painting the Earth with a brilliant muse.

Each petal a note, in a beautiful melody
Woven in a warm embrace
In every rustle, each shining ray
The forest sings softly, inviting us to stay.

As you wander deeper where the magic lives,
In the heart of the forest, it endlessly gives,
With each heartbeat, nature takes its course
Flowing like rivers, in beauty, we soar.

In the hush of dawn, where rivers flow
Whispers of water in a gentle glow
They sparkle and dance in love with the breeze
Carrying secrets beneath the tall trees.

Flowers sway softly like a colourful parade
Petals and bushes the sun has made dancing
With rhythm, with the river's song
In a vibrant world where we all belong.

Willows, where gracefully their branches sweep low
Painting the banks with a lush green show
Sunlight kisses leaves like laughter on streams
In a world full of nature's dreams.

So here's to the magic the beauty we see.
Flowing with life each twist a work of art
Let's wander the trails where the wild spirits roam
And immerse ourselves in nature, our one true home.

Jemimah Mohammed (13)
Stantonbury High School, Stantonbury

The Past That Lay Forgotten

Upon that hill with fields so wide,
The grass stands tall beneath the winter sky,
The rising storm will seldom subside,
And the soaring winds howl as they pass by.

The frosty air leaves a bitter taste,
And the trees stand bare an inch from death,
The haunted screams of a thousand men lay barefaced,
And noses are filled with a foul odour like that of a dragon's breath.

The decaying roof barely holds, afraid and alone,
Yet still remains the only hope for the splintering wood and fractured clay,
And as the house and trees forever sway, the mailbox stands as if made of stone,
As it houses memories upon memories, clear as day.

The clouds hang low towards the quivering ground,
They cry endless tears that never quite seem to dry,
The darkened sky surrounds every corner, all around,
Every inch of land resents the sun above who has long since waved goodbye.

Alone and helpless, I struggled with all my might,
Desperately clinging to all those who have long since passed,
My walls, once filled with joy, cheer and light,
Now crumpled broodingly, endlessly downcast.

Every step that graced my beloved grounds was a haven to my heart,
Far too long had it been since I had been embraced with longing and loving arms,
The portraits that once littered my caring walls, embodiments of art,
Now lie shattered, strewn along my forgotten floor like dead bodies with a thousand burns.

The strings of nature had long ago taken to strangling me with their decorative vines,
The graves of my loved ones so close yet so far, haunting me for evermore,
All but a blistering breeze could reach within my confines,
The paws of the howling wolf pressed hard against the dry grassy floor.

I stood on the edge of collapse, fragile and exposed,
My body trembled beneath the strenuous weight, ready to give way,
Despair and exhaustion creeping within my bricks, barely in control,
A forgotten relic stuck in the past with no one to cease my slow decay.

I hummed a melancholy tune at the sight of what once was,
This marvellous creation reduced to nothing but sticks and stones,
This once scenic land that was fading without cause,
The very thought irked me to my very bones.

The Beautiful Truth - The Hope Of Tomorrow

This place of which I had once called my home,
A childlike laughter filled every room,
Yet now fear demanded respect like a king upon his throne,
A home without love or hearth, a place of endless gloom.

Here I sat, tied to the ground on which I once stood,
Eternally remembered through flowers and grief,
My soul alive yet my heart buried deep, lost and misunderstood,
Wincing at the knowledge of what time really is; a thief.

Yearning for a semblance of warmth,
In this hell of isolation and contempt,
As cold as a night up in the north,
My soul freezes over; a pathetic attempt.

'Time is an illusion',
Is it true or not?
Am I merely a delusion; the heart of your confusion,
Or am I the reality that leaves one oh so distraught?

The plants will wilt as winter comes,
Humanity will age with every passing day,
The old will die leaving but meagre crumbs,
The house will fall and tear away.

They find me evil, a despicable beast,
Yet what is there to love if all is infinite and unchanging?
I am your nightmares yet also your hopes and dreams released,
What is there to life, without my intervening?

And as the wind whispers through hollowed walls,
Time leaves its trace but speaks no name,
The past sleeps in dust, forgotten and still,
A story unravelled, yet never reclaimed.

Jannat Rashid (15)
Stantonbury High School, Stantonbury

Dance Of The Seasons

Spring's samba leaps across the breeze,
Shaking and flowing skirts of trees,
Mother Nature steps with a twirl,
Emerald leaves will now unfurl.

Summer's heat brings a tango beat,
And Mother Nature taps her feet,
As flowers grow ever higher,
They bloom in deeper shades of fire.

On dappled forest floors of gold,
Our Mother Nature's tales are told,
Autumn foxtrots around the trees,
In the form of marigold leaves.

Mother Nature changes her gown,
Laced in webs as snowflakes fall down,
Her icy breath flows through the night,
Stars twinkle with a frosty light.

Yet hidden deep within her fears,
Lies the truth over changing years,
As climate change darkens the skies,
Tears prick her heartbroken eyes,
Nature weeps for what is lost,
A sign of what humans can cost.

Lanie Hanbidge-Moore
The Castle School, Taunton

Starry Sadness

In the velvet cloak of night,
Stars gleam bright,
Whispers of the cosmos dance in silver light,
The moon, a lantern, casts a gentle glow,
Guiding dreams and secrets that only night can know,
Constellations weave tales of old,
Heroes and legends in the darkness told,
The Milky Way, a river of shimmering dust,
Holds the universe's wonders, a sight we trust,
As the night deepens, the world feels still,
A tranquil silence that gives the heart a thrill,
So I gaze upon the heavens, and let my spirit fly,
For in the vastness of the night, we all touch the sky,
But I know me, and only I,
Can hear the stars bellow and cry,
Whilst others see shades of purple, blue and black,
I see streaks of light following a track,
And in the quiet of the night, the sky unfolds,
A tapestry of thoughts is controlled,
Stars like diamonds scattered far and wide,
Whispering secrets, where the mysteries hide,
The moon hangs low, a guardian bright,
Casting soft shadows, bathing all in light,

But this one star stays in the sky,
And it has the loudest cry,
All the light around it will eventually bend,
I am afraid, or nervous, to call this star my only friend.

Harvey Yarde (12)
The Castle School, Taunton

The Bittersweet

Aromas waft through the thin, calm air,
The earthy smell of digging peat,
Fragrances of bitterness linger with a stare,
The lovely taste of the bittersweet,
It burns my mouth and in my lungs,
Art created and then destroyed,
A beautiful song that is sung,
Of all emotion it is void,
All my energy has long depleted,
My social battery has run dry,
My whole life left uncompleted,
And all I want is to try,
Try to fly, try to treat,
Try to taste that bittersweet.

Sounds of silence ring through my ear,
My hand burns from the wear and tear,
The ticking hands make me form a single tear,
With all the regrets that I wear,
Bells echo throughout the room,
I feel the clashing silver stop,
And all I dig will become my tomb,
While my cup fills to the top,
I want to be free, to be rid of this,
But the shackles of the tick, tick, ticking keep me here,
I wish I could fly, on clouds of bliss,

But evermore, I still trip on my fear,
What I would give to try to soar, try to face defeat,
Try to taste that bittersweet.

Arlo Norbury (12)
The Castle School, Taunton

Masking

What mask should I wear today?
What is the expectation?
To swallow down the one inside and cause more confrontation

What mask should I adopt right now?
Whilst inside my heart is pacing
I cannot show the inside or the reality I'm facing

Should I grin and bear right through?
Should I bury down deep within
All the true emotions
Hide the stuff that lurks herein

If I adorn my face with calm contemplation
Will the tight knot in my chest
Remain coldly anonymous
And not call others to invest

What mask should go on socials?
No one wants to hear me vent
A look of success and triumph
To give the impression I'm content

What mask should I leave at home?
One filled with tears and frustration?
Put my stiff upper lip on.
It is, after all, the way of this 'great' nation

When am I safe to freely show
All the ways I feel below
The everyday facade I must upkeep
To keep all emotions locked in deep
Never should I cause a scene
And reveal the faces I have been.

Elliott O'Shea (13)
The Castle School, Taunton

Climate Change

Nature's cradle, where I find my peace,
Beneath the leaves, my stresses cease,
Up in the sky, above my head,
The birds sing sweet, the clouds lay dead.

Wildflowers grow, in the meadows' chorus,
While busy buzzing bees, share their truths,
Little bouncy bunnies, hop to and fro,
While delicate dancing deer, leap over hedges.

But alas, that fateful day,
A threat to the leaves, the trees, the mud,
The rising temperatures, the scorching summer sun,
A wake-up call, an unforgivable truth.

The ice caps melt, the water levels rise,
The gardens sink, the animals die,
The atmosphere crumples, the Earth cries
A loss of homes, a loss of time.

But wait a second, all is not lost,
There is a way, there's a chance,
To do what's right, to change our ways
We can do it, it's never too late.

So we shall act, we shall think
Let's save our Earth, let's create a future
If we don't change soon, bad things will come,
It's time to unite, time to save everyone.

Mia Lewis
The Castle School, Taunton

Brown To Blonde

She changed her hair
Her clothes
Her laugh
She changed even more than that

She changed her personality
Her shoes
Her dreams
But it was false as can be

She was not happy, she was in misery
When she looked in the mirror, the face was not hers
Some perfect girl she did not know
With a pretty face and smile

She was still lonely, depressed and sad
But behind a shield of blonde hair, glitter, pink, glitz and glam
Perfect, popular and pretty; her dream came true

She was perfect before; her brown hair
Her green eyes, freckles and glasses
Smart, strong and kind
She was trying to fit into the wrong group of people, plastic and fake, manipulative and mean.

She was bullied but now the bully
She looked in the mirror
And said to herself
This is not me. Who is that girl looking at me?

Olivia-Rose Wibrew (12)
The Castle School, Taunton

Nothing

Flooding. Wildfires. Drought.
It's become normal to hear these things on the news,
What are we doing about it?
Nothing.

We can say things are changing,
We can set ourselves high targets,
But what if we don't reach them?
Nothing. Nothing will change.

We can set ourselves new targets,
Say this time we'll get it right,
But what difference is 'saying it' gonna make?
Nothing. We have to act.

There is no use in protesting for change,
We must use our time well,
Because what are placards gonna do in the long run?
Nothing, we have to act.

It doesn't matter if you're young or you're old.
It doesn't matter if you're rich or you're poor.
The truth isn't beautiful; it's ugly,
And without change it will only get worse.

Ava Taylor (12)
The Castle School, Taunton

My Poem

The cold wind blows as a machine gun mows.
Pitter-patter goes the rain while shells roar away.
Water flows in the boots and shoes of those who are smug,
And in the mind of the defunct.

A shrill whistle plays out over the horizon,
And cries of freedom tear away.

The ground rumbles,
The bullets echo,
And grenades get hurled like snowballs.

The enemy barrages through the resistance,
And all morale has gone by.

Atrocities are committed in the trenches,
And the pleading of the defenceless are disregarded.

Stabbings occur,
The wounded are gunned,
And the rest are torched with flippancy.

They have failed to secure their territory.
They will be dishonoured and bygone.
Their nation crumbles in defeat.

The battle has concluded.

Viren Peter (12)
The Castle School, Taunton

Just Think

Just think if we grew more trees
Just think if we wandered under the cool breeze
Just think if we stopped and thought
Just think if we remembered all the battles we fought

Just think of the icebergs melting away
Just think of the trees turning grey
Just think of the seas rising high
Just think of the animals who slowly die

Just think of the air, thick with despair
Just think of the future that needs to be repaired
Just think of the rivers clear and bright
Just think of the stars shining in the clear night

Just think of the consequences our choices make
Just think of all the changes that we could create
Just think of the sky clear and free
Just think of all the beautiful flowers and bees.

Alice Farmer (12)
The Castle School, Taunton

The Beautiful Truth

People just do not do very much
People just do not do what they need
People just do not help their brother
Maybe today was going to be their day

   D on't stop to give up
   R ealise what you love to do
   E ventually it'll be me and you
   A dream is all that anyone has got
   M aybe today was going to be the day

People just do not do very much
People just do not do what they need
People just do not help their brother
Maybe today was going to be their day

   D o what people say
   R eally we need people, you
   E xactly when will you start to care
   A dream is all that anyone has got
   M aybe today still is, in fact, your day.

Manny Ashley (13)
The Castle School, Taunton

Outside Vs Inside

It's not about what you wear or the kind or type of hair
It's about what's inside that counts
It doesn't matter where you're from or who you want to become
It's what's inside that counts
It doesn't matter who you prefer, if you like him or her
It's about what's inside that counts
It doesn't matter if you have a disability, it is part of your individuality
It's about what's inside that counts
It's not about your faith or religion, you are still one in eight billion
It's about what's inside that counts
You shouldn't change for anyone or anything
We are all different and unique and that's what makes us all special
It's okay to be you.

Amandine Playfair
The Castle School, Taunton

Football

Football is not just a game
It can bring joy to many people's lives
It can be fuel for aims
And boosts lots of young people's strives
Football is not just about kicking a ball
It's much more than that it makes you stand tall
When you nutmeg the defender you've got a clear chance of shooting
You better not miss or you're going to get a booting
The desire, the energy, the dopamine rush
The keeper is shivering, his legs turned to mush
Dribbling past everyone
Shooting and scoring
Missing a penalty
You make it look boring
Football is not just a game
The teamwork, the determination, and winning again and again.

Artie Townsend
The Castle School, Taunton

Fire

Fire, flame, that which burns
Man's first dream,
Find it writes in black, in a scorching ink,
For the stitches of our souls,
The binding to our minds,
And to bend such things upon themselves.

The warmth and light, one shared dream,
But never had one however,
Found such awful substance,
Which created one's true firstborn
Nightmare.

The destruction and passion, one shared fear,
To dance and teeter, swallow and force,
Would be one's first thought,
The daring, fighting sorrow.
So think,
Fire, flame, that which burns,
A blood-red feeling, a voice whispering,
Remember me.

Bella Snailham
The Castle School, Taunton

Don't Keep It A Secret

This is our world, our home, but we
Are destroying it in, one, two, three
It's not a secret, everyone knows

So, let's work together to help and resolve
The job needs passion and everyone to care
But if you don't, your future will not be there

Don't keep it a secret, tell everyone you know that we need to do this together to create a new home

Pick up your rubbish and tell your friends
Do what you can to create change
We all need to do this, or the effect won't be the same

Don't keep it a secret, tell everyone you know that we need to do this together to create a new home.

Abigail Collings
The Castle School, Taunton

October

October is a time of change, a forgotten month we forget to arrange
Falling leaves once bright and green are now dancing colours, like a blanket of dreams
The fruit and nuts begin to fall, squirrels and mice gathering all
In a hollow of moss and wood, songs are sung of times understood
Quilts wrap us up warmly in their cosy, colourful hold
While fireside embers dance in tales of days old
In anticipation for the bells' chime, of Christmas cheer, mince pies and wine
And so it seems to pass us by, however hard we seem to try
The world is not yet a blanket of white, there is still time for a real good fright.

Rosie Huxtable-Curno
The Castle School, Taunton

The Farm

To the east of the town
Just over the hill
The sunlight, a crown
Shining over this mill

And here at the mill
Lies a tranquil, old farm
The quiet of the dawn
Brings a deep sense of calm

But as the sun rises
The cattle they stir
The frost on their field
And the dew on their fur

With a spring in their step
The lambs skip along
They call out to their mothers
With a sweet tender song

The paths through the farm
Blanketed in crisp, copper leaves
Are a sea of ochre foliage
Here the autumn air breathes.

Beatrice Nicholson (13)
The Castle School, Taunton

Climate Change

Whirlwinds, hurricanes, floods,
Droughts, deserts, disasters,
Cold, snow, ice.
Help, we are running out of time.

Fires raging through the forests,
Tsunamis crashing at the shores,
Torrential downpours of rain.
Help, we are running out of time.

Ice caps melting, sea levels rising,
Forests falling, animals dying,
World heating, illnesses spreading.
Help, we are running out of time.

But...
This is not all set in stone,
This can change.
Together, we can change the course of our Earth.
Help, we might have enough time.

Hannah Gilling (13)
The Castle School, Taunton

The Power Of Friendship

In a quiet yard where the sun shines bright
A boy and his dog share pure delight
With a wagging tail and a playful bark
They chase through the grass, leaving their mark
Together they roam, side by side
In fields of laughter, their hearts open wide
Through muddy puddles and trees so tall
In each other's company, they have it all
At the end of the day, as the stars appear
The boy whispers softly, "I'm glad you're here"
For in every adventure, come rain or shine
The love of a boy and his dog is divine.

Emerson Goss (13)
The Castle School, Taunton

The Freedom Of The Midnight

As she winds through the shadows
Gone are all her past worries and sorrows

Running, tumbling, the moon as her guide
Heart pounding fast with spring in her stride

The city's in slumber as she weaves through the streets
The silence so quiet, how simply so sweet

Her flowing long hair, shines in the stars of the sky
Her mind feels free as the world passes by

With each everlasting step she takes, she feels herself grow strong
In the silence of the midnight, where she truly belongs.

Gabriella Lawton (12)
The Castle School, Taunton

Life And Sound

The flowers opened their eyes,
And watched the sun rise,
The grass was covered in morning dew,
The butterflies said nothing as they flew.

The birds started singing their morning tune,
The trees started dancing with the morning breeze,
The air started buzzing with busy bees,
The bunnies hopped out of their little home.

The hedgehogs scampered on the ground,
The ants went hunting for food,
Waiting to be found,
The world is filled with life and sound.

Elena Kontopoulos
The Castle School, Taunton

The Truth

The truth is always the right thing
To do
But sometimes the truth can hurt
A lot too
Others say the truth is the wrong thing
To do
But sometimes the truth can benefit
You too.

Sometimes the truth is knowing when
You have failed
But sometimes failure is also
The truth
And some people might say that when
You lie
You are sneaky and sly to get out of trouble
But when you lie
The truth will always come back and
Haunt you!

Hayden Yarde (13)
The Castle School, Taunton

The Beautiful Game

From the first whistle to the last,
You run, you tackle, you shoot, you pass
With skill and elegance, you glide over the field,
Dancing past defenders, your talent revealed,
Showing speed and passion, toil and sweat,
With the flick of your foot, the ball hits the net,
From the highs in victory to the lows in defeat,
You never give up with the ball at your feet,
It's a game for all to come together,
Making memories that will last forever.

Josh Hawkins
The Castle School, Taunton

Wintertime

Snow falls gently to the ground
Coating the world with no sound
Cold winds howl on winter's night
Stars twinkle ever so bright

Frosty mornings, skies are dark
Shorter hours in the day
Warmth is found in family hugs
With hot chocolate and fires so bright

Nature sleeps, covered in snow
Patiently waiting for the sun's warm glow
Winter's beauty, peaceful and still
The best season is such a thrill.

Grace Walker
The Castle School, Taunton

My Favourite Pet

I love my dog with all my heart
even when we are apart.

The ripping of towels
the stealing of socks
he's been by my side
since having chickenpox.

The walks are wild
the kisses are wet
but he has proved
he'll be my favourite pet.

The brown fluffy coat
the huge padded paws
we love him still
through all his flaws.

I love my dog with all my heart
even when we are apart.

Lucy Bernard (13)
The Castle School, Taunton

Ode To Haikus

Haiku poetry

I can't write poems
Find them challenging to write
But I like haikus

Haikus are helpful
They give me structure and fun
They get the task done

Limericks could work
To inspire my thought process
But my brain has ceased

I could write an ode
Although Shakespeare would explode
Oh how thee would wode

For me, haikus win
There is no competition
Here is my haiku.

Edith Watson
The Castle School, Taunton

The Man On The Moon

Did a man go to the moon?
Or was he just a silly old loon?
If we had the right tech then
Why can't we just go again?

So tell me why, so tell me why?
This could all just be a lie.
The trip did in fact take quite long.
So I could just be in the wrong!

So did a man go to the moon?
Or was he just a silly old loon?
So as I sit here on the roof,
I still feel like we need more proof!

Ned Parkes (12)
The Castle School, Taunton

Time Is Running Out

Haiku poetry

Beautiful coral,
Bright underwater forest,
Fishes swimming free.

Our world is dying,
Bleached corals surround the sea,
Danger lies ahead.

Amazing blossom,
Flowers blooming in the sun,
Glistening oceans.

A graveyard of trees,
Animals losing their homes,
Fire spreads quickly.

We need to act now,
To save our bright, precious world,
Time is running out.

Amy Vautier (12)
The Castle School, Taunton

I Don't Like Homework

I don't like homework
But I don't have a choice
Because if I don't do it I get in trouble
It takes up all my time
And then it's time to sleep
And then I don't have time
To do anything but eat
If I don't bring it in
I still have to do it at a later date
I'd much rather do all I want
And play games all day
Rather than pointless homework
Every single day.

Sebastian Ivan
The Castle School, Taunton

The Beach

T wirling seaweed stuck on your feet,
H undreds of people sunbathing in the heat,
E verlasting memories lay in this bay,

B eautiful view from far away,
E ating fish and chips on their stay,
A ll the dogs bounding around,
C hildren building sandcastles on the sandy ground,
H eavy crashing waves pound at the sand making a monstrous sound.

Jesse Sweeting (13)
The Castle School, Taunton

The Final Heartbeat

The final heartbeat fades
Nature's hand reclaims the glade
Life's cycle starts anew

Vines creep overdone
Wildflowers bloom, brightly shone
Beauty rising from loss

In silence, breath holds tight
Echoes of what once felt right
As shadows dance in peace

Yet in this stillness
Life's essence finds its sweetness
A promise of new life.

Kevin Dela Cruz
The Castle School, Taunton

Time For Change

E nergy from carbon
N o concern for our future
V oila, the world is getting too hot
I cebergs melting, becoming water
R ivers rising, flooding towns
O ceans filling with our plastic
N o concern for our future
M other Nature in despair
E ver increasing fire
N o concern for our future
T ime for change.

Arran McDonald (13)
The Castle School, Taunton

Untitled

It's wintertime, family time
Dark nights and snowy daytimes
Icicles drip from rooftops
And hang from swaying trees
All I can see is fallen leaves

It's wintertime, family time
I love winter. Christmas is sublime
You get to celebrate with family and great friends
Opening presents - I hope this good fun never ends
Christmas, please come quick again!

Amber Biggs (12)
The Castle School, Taunton

Music

Music,
Loud and heavy,
Calm and quiet,
Softly spoken words of magic,
Strummed on guitar or slammed on drums,
Different for everyone,
For the small, for the big,
There's more and more the deeper you dig,
Emotional, happy, angry,
There's a song for everyone,
Fast, slow, whatever it takes,
A part of our life through and through.

Joshua Griffiths (12)
The Castle School, Taunton

The Weather

English weather is typical,
Rain, sun or storm,
It's always wet, always cloudy,
You could say it's predictable,
When it's wet, look for the warm
And if it's ever warm,
Enjoy it while you can,

English weather is typical,
You always feel the cold,
So enjoy it now,
Embrace the cold,
Enjoy it till you're old.

Daniel Brown (12)
The Castle School, Taunton

The Truth About Truth

A truth is something,
That is factually true,
It could make you smile,
It could leave you feeling blue.

But what about lies,
We all know we aren't meant to,
But a little lie,
Is never going to hurt.

The truth is very good,
So we should live by the truth,
But sometimes we need to lie,
To protect the truth.

Alfie Prince
The Castle School, Taunton

My Poem

My dog is dying, it breaks my heart,
He's been there for me from the start.
He's tired and old,
His story's nearly been told.
I'll cry when he goes,
End up shaking from head to toes.
I'll miss him forever,
No one can say never.
My dog is dying, it breaks my heart,
He's been there for me, since the very start.

Lacey Bishop (13)
The Castle School, Taunton

Untitled

In a sunlit yard where laughter plays,
A boy and his dog spend endless days,
With fur so soft, a warm embrace,
Together they run, a joyful chase.

Through fields they wander, touching sides,
Time goes suddenly and quickly flies,
With wagging tails and souls so free,
A bond unbroken, just him and his pup, you see.

Zack Coles (13)
The Castle School, Taunton

Enough

Haiku poetry

To be in the world
Do you have to be enough,
Or can you be you?

Do you have to fit
Like the people around you,
Or can it fit you?

If you know the truth
Are you just left believing,
Good will come to you?

What goes on inside
Is not for others to see,
But for you to dream.

Anya Shearman (12)
The Castle School, Taunton

Queen Of The Night

In the forest where shadows creep,
A one-eyed cat she softly leaps.
With fur so dark and eye so bright,
The moon will guide her through the night.

Gentle steps on autumn leaves,
Through the trees a midnight breeze.
Her single eye, a ray of light,
My one-eyed cat, queen of the night.

Pippa Parrish (13)
The Castle School, Taunton

Imperfection

The things that shape you are not your
Victories but your failures
Embrace failure and victory will arrive
Imperfection is the perfect solution
A wise man said, "The actions you do, speak louder than the words you say."
Nature is not perfect, but nature is beautiful
Be your natural self.

Hayden McMurdo (13)
The Castle School, Taunton

My Cat

In the sun's glow, she walks with grace
A queen on her throne, her favourite place
With a flick of the tail and a regal glance
She rules the house with just a glance

Paws on the counter, she knows every place
Demanding dinner with a soft face.

Frederick Paul
The Castle School, Taunton

Beautiful Truths

Beautiful truths are precious and bright
They help us see what's wrong with what's right
In every smile, it's all so clear
The truth is magic, always near!
We need to be honest, kind and true
So beautiful truths shine in me and you.

Mina Leslie
The Castle School, Taunton

About Me

An early riser.
A kind brother.
A sports player.
A cricket fan.
A music master.
A homework hater.
A snack eater.
A Lego lover.
A rapid runner.
A tennis server.
A book reader.
A car knower.

Alexander Hingley (13)
The Castle School, Taunton

Even When I'm Sad
A haiku

Even when I'm sad
You make me so overjoyed
Like the sun rising.

Annabelle Hall (12)
The Castle School, Taunton

Defining Pride

I am not defined by those around me
I am not defined by the things I can't see
I am not defined by the things I can't reach
I am not defined by the things only my teachers teach.

I want to learn
I want to gain knowledge
I want to strive for progress
I want to know things I don't know
And constantly grow
And fill those around me and myself with pride.

Pride is a concept that is new to some
It is not a notion that all know
It is up to me to be the best I can be
And uphold the values that John Roan endorse
I want to see the best in everyone
but most of all, I want to see the best in me!

Respecting our differences and our diversity
Is an important part of life at John Roan
It's up to all of us to be kind and caring
And look after one another, no matter what
I will always respect my teachers and peers
And I know they will respect me.

Being *Involved* in our work
Reflecting on our actions
And being good citizens
Of John Roan, Blackheath and London
This is another value I uphold
And involve myself in school life each day.

Determined each day to be on time
I set my alarm extra early
I want to start each day with a smile
And go the extra mile
To reach the goals that are set
I want to do my best to uphold
The ethos and values
Of The John Roan School.

Excellent is how I've found my start
To school life here at John Roan
It's certainly a change from primary school
But I was ready for it
Aiming for excellence each and every day
Is something that burns inside
It gives me an incentive to work hard
Do my best in all I do
And it fills me with pride.

George Hodgins (11)
The John Roan School, Blackheath

Whispers Of Night

In whispers of dawn, where
The light breaks anew,
The beautiful truth lies in
Moments so true.
In laughter and tears, in the
Warmth of a smile,
In the embrace of the earth
In each verdant mile.

It dances in shadows, in the
Hush of the night,
In the gleam of the stars, it
Ignites silent light.
Amidst the chaos, where the
Wild rivers flow,
The beautiful truth is in all
That we know.

It's found in the kindness, in
A stranger's warm glance,
In the rhyme of life, in the
Delicate dance.
In dreams yet to chase and
The hopes yet to sing,
The beautiful truth is the joy
That we bring.

It's woven into stories, in the
Pages we turn,
In the fires of passion, in the
Lessons we learn.
A tapestry rich with threads
Soft and bold,
The beautiful truth is a
Treasure to hold.

So let us decipher the
Whispers so clear,
In the heartbeat of silence
Let love draw us near.
Embrace every moment, let
Your spirit take flight,
For the beautiful truth
Shines most brilliantly bright.

Artem Baliuk (13)
The John Roan School, Blackheath

Truth In School

When I wake up, I dread it -
The constant, never-ending lessons of 100 minutes!
"Are they 100 minutes long, truly?"
True - they torture us and make us sit for that long!

When again it's Monday, I dread it -
The constant never-ending line-ups - four a day!
"Four? Truly?"
True - they make us stand in the cold for fifteen minutes at a time!

After the weekend, I dread it -
The short, clipped bits of happiness in the short breaks
Only two - one twenty minutes and one forty-five!
"That short? Truly?"
True - and the lunch line's so long, I barely get time to eat!

When it comes round again, I dread it -
The 6:30 wake-ups and detention for losing a pencil!
"6:30? And detention for losing a pencil?"
True - so petty, so sad, so annoying!

So when I go to bed...
I cry, hoping for change that will never come...

Morgan Reynolds (11)
The John Roan School, Blackheath

It Is Who I Am

I like cats,
They are soft.
Like my sleep,
It is nice.
It is who I am,
The person right here.

I am sad,
No one is near me.
Alone in my room,
Music is my therapy
It is who I am,
The person right here.

I smile.
I'm happy
With my friends.
They make me happy.
It is who I am,
The person right here.

I am me,
The one that is kind.
I am me,
The one that is quiet.
It is who I am,
The person right here.

Zoja Woloszyn (13)
The John Roan School, Blackheath

The Real Earth

Sunset lies whisper for my eyes;
Logic succumbs to the moon.
Fail, have multiple tries,
You'll always be able to return.

Moonlight rays scatter the truth;
Heart beating with the planet.
Extend beyond your booth,
Don't place bets.

Ocean tides crash and burn,
Speak the word,
Repost at every turn,
Follow the birds.

Midnight rains extinguish,
Nurture the water,
Served on a silver dish,
No more martyrs!

James Mac (15)
The John Roan School, Blackheath

I Have A Cat

I have a cat
He is fat
He is hungry
He is sad

He eats a lot
He sleeps a lot
He drinks a lot
He plays a lot

I have a cat
I like my cat
He is cute
He is fat.

Rugile Kazakeviciute (13)
The John Roan School, Blackheath

The Truth Is Never Told

The truth is never told
People lie to me every day
I can't trust anyone
Or anything they say

Everyone fights to be heard
People always think they are right
But under all of the decay and mould
They are just people who forgot to be kind

Now, the countries are lonely
There is no peace just war
This world has so much tragedy
The base is torn

We have to live with the thought
That there is death and horrid laws
That people may never get better
And sometimes not even pause

But maybe we can fix this
Our generation has hope
We need to change this world
So the truth can be told

So we should build the base up
Make the world a better place
Stop all of these wars
And end the cheating race

Break limits and set free
Extinguish the blazing storms
And become the people who make sure
That the truth is always told.

Aditi Sharma (13)
The Peterborough School, Peterborough

What Am I, If Not A Lie?

What am I, if not a lie?
The perfect person, weaving laughter
And words with their friends.
Hiding their cards under their skin.
The academic achiever,
The pride of their teachers.
Trying to bury away from their lives
Under chemical formulas.
The bookworm,
Who travels endlessly through stories
To dodge their own truth.
The artistic student,
Who wishes no more than to slip quietly
Into the darkness woven of their own strokes.
The music lover,
Who lets the music weave through their body
To block out the loudness of their own head.
The athlete,
Who tries to outrun the whispers
Of the storm that is their mind.
What am I, if not a lie?

Avika Yadav (13)
The Peterborough School, Peterborough

Roll Up! Roll Up!

A m I good at this?
M aybe I am,
B eing an ambassador for our school, telling the truth at
A ll times.
S elling a dream,
S elling a school,
A bove and beyond expectations.
D ance, drama, science, and maths are all on
O ffer
R oll up! Roll up! Come to school open evening!

Alina Jack-Price (16)
The Vyne Community School, Basingstoke

Our Beautiful Truth

Wipe those puddles of tears that have collected on your screen,
This iridescent surface glow shouldn't control your regime,
Let the natural world's vines and leaves,
Grow and spread, covering these words so mean,
Know that their pain and power isn't real and can be easily swept clean,
With confidence in our wonderful planet,
Sky blue and plant stems green.

In this modern world, people are so focused on their selfies and Snapchat streaks,
That they could go on receiving all this input for many hours, days and weeks,
Not knowing this world can make them feel weak,
Like everyone's thriving and you'll never reach the peak
Of the mountain of pressure that is put on us humans,
To live up to a set of standards surely not made for humans,
But for immortal, celestial, fantasy creatures,
who really can have it all,
Not real-life people who make mistakes and can often drop the ball,
And then beat ourselves up for not being as good as those people on TV,
And wish that someday, we could find their secret recipe.

But these hopes and dreams are fake and cruel,
They destroy who we really are,
You are unique,
You are beautiful,
Like a night sky full of shining stars.

So let a starlight white ocean wave crest glow,
Take over the light of your untruthful phone,
And reach for the sky,
Don't let people ask why,
And know that you're never alone.

Lara Hopkins (13)
Thomas Keble School, Eastcombe

The Black Rose

In the middle of the chilly grassland,
Lies a mysterious artefact,
More glistening than sapphires,
Concealed in an icy tomb,
Touch its warm petals,
It is surrounded by the monotonous company of rocks,
Inhale a fragrance so sweet,
Almost like the pleasant scent of musk,
The picturesque sight,
More ravishing than a patch of chrysanthemums,
Shades of numerous flowers,
Sway in solitude,
Confidential, nonchalant,
Not a thing compared to the rose,
Absence of colour,
Stem like the lacy wings of an angel,
The sky is a sleek, silky chest,
Concealing beauty,
An intimate and restful blanket,
Stinging nettles stand,
File-barked trees,
This factor never at ease,
Sweeping leaves, golden reds and browns,
Bitter crunches,
Winter, summer, autumn, spring,

A never or ever,
Possibly a happy ending,
Wither or hither,
Towards the sombre,
Uninviting place,
Lies and object which
Should never go to
Waste.

Javeria Kamran (11)
Twickenham School, Whitton

The Yee Woo Crossroads

At the Yee Woo crossroads, the city hums
A collection of memories where the heartbeat drums
The bustling crowds covered by the reflection of the light
The neon signs speak to me, painting the night

The air is thick with the fragrant scent of delight
Street vendors calling, with their treasures in sight
From the spicy meat skewers to the sweet bubble tea
Each stall, a story that fills me with glee

The trams glide past, moving in a steady flow
The lights from the cars giving the city a picturesque glow
A symphony of voices, all singing aloud
At the crossroads, where there's always a crowd

As the twilight deepens, the lanterns glow bright
Casting warm shadows dancing in the night
In the heart of the chaos, there's beauty to find
A pulse of Hong Kong, where all paths intertwine.

Emily Hall (13)
Twickenham School, Whitton

Friendship

To have a friend like you
It doesn't feel real
In a world full of darkness
Your encouragement is a beam of light
You never give up on me
You inspire me to follow my dreams
Your smile is as warm as the sun shining down on me
You're always helpful and supportive
You're important, my friend
I'm proud to know you.

Chloe Ku (13)
Twickenham School, Whitton

Tiger

T ame and calm, the cat lay down
I ntelligent and imaginative, the furry friend wondered
G raceful and generous, he loved all his family
E ager and intrigued, he always wanted to know what was happening
R adiant soft fur and magnificent eyes, he was always there to lend his paw to anyone - I love you, Tiger.

Ocearna Harvey-Bullock (15)
Wellfield Community School, Wingate

No Happy Endings

There are no happy endings,
Endings are the saddest part,
So just give me a happy middle,
And a very happy start.

Kaitlyn-Louise Gorton (12)
Wellfield Community School, Wingate

The Beautiful Truth

The black, shiny plastic.
The cushiony fabric against my ears.
I lengthen the band to fit around my head.
I turn them on.

I feel the back of my earrings against the sides of my head
Adjust the headphones so they're comfy.
I pull my phone out of my jeans' pocket,
And scroll through my songs.

Before I tap on a playlist,
I make sure they are connected.
I press 'shuffle'
And the songs play.

From rock to pop,
And indie to rap,
I look out the car window,
As the world whirrs by.

It nearly blocks out the background noise
The negative pile I'll flick through later
My parents laughing and chuckling from the podcasts they listen to
The rucksack of stress is set down
Letting me savour this moment
Just my music and I

Turning the volume up ever so slightly,
I listen to the beat, the lyrics, quietly,
In the back of the car.

Eleanor Goodwin (13)
Wellington College, Belfast

The Tunnel To Croke Park

The day has come
The day I've been training for since I was eight
All the injuries, all the times I thought about giving up
They've all led up to today
Surrounded by my teammates, my second family
Our hearts thumping in our chests
Will we win? Will I make a difference?
Will I make my granda proud?
All these thoughts race each other for number one in my head, just like us
However, the most important thing is that my granda is out there
Painted in my county colours
Ready to cheer me on to victory
I must make him proud
This is it
I hear the muffled roar of the crowd
Knowing my granda is one of those voices
I run alongside my teammates
Our studs clicking on the hard concrete floor
Time's up
Let's play.

Erin Carr (12)
Wellington College, Belfast

The Beautiful Truth

I lay my back onto the garments of my bed
Quietly my mind unweaves
A tangled mess of questions
Who am I?
It rings through my brain
Where do I fit in the ones and zeros?
I see through the eyes of man and woman alike
However neither feel like my own
I use my eyes
Staring upon the stars in my head.

I take three deep breaths
One, two, three
The music in my ears blasts
Distracting myself from my thoughts
I can relax, for now
Until I ask the question again
Who am I?

Clara Toal
Wellington College, Belfast

YOUNG WRITERS INFORMATION

We hope you have enjoyed reading this book – and that you will continue to in the coming years.

If you're the parent or family member of an enthusiastic poet or story writer, do visit our website **www.youngwriters.co.uk/subscribe** and sign up to receive news, competitions, writing challenges and tips, activities and much, much more! There's lots to keep budding writers motivated!

If you would like to order further copies of this book, or any of our other titles, then please give us a call or order via your online account.

Young Writers
Remus House
Coltsfoot Drive
Peterborough
PE2 9BF
(01733) 890066
info@youngwriters.co.uk

**Join in the conversation!
Tips, news, giveaways and much more!**

YoungWritersUK   YoungWritersCW

youngwriterscw   youngwriterscw